Advance Praise for *The Next Superpower?*

"Having worked closely with Ambassador Schnabel during my term as President of the European Parliament I can attest to the pivotal role which he played in the vital arena of EU-U.S. relations. This book is testimony to his insider witness and feel, and a convincing argument that the best option for the future of both Europe and America is one of intelligent interdependence."

— **Pat Cox**, Former President, European Parliament

"The task of revitalizing the Atlantic alliance is one of the highest priorities for American foreign policy. Only by restoring a sense of common purpose to history's most successful coalition of free-market democracies can the Bush administration achieve its lofty ambition of spreading freedom around the world. Nobody understands this mission better than Rockwell Schnabel, who has served with great distinction in difficult times as the United States ambassador to the European Union. This book explains why transatlantic rivalry is self-defeating and how Europe and America must rebuild their partnership to succeed in coping with the economic and security challenges of the twenty-first century."

— **William M. Drozdiak**, President, American Council on Germany, and Former Foreign Editor, *The Washington Post*

"*The Next Superpower?* is one of the most important books ever written about the European Union, one of the least understood but most important institutions in the world. From an inside perspective, as America's widely respected ambassador to the European Union, Rockwell Schnabel clearly and convincingly explains, in ways few have done, how the EU works; its crucial economic and political impacts; the need to support a strong, unified Europe; and the critical importance to U.S. economic and security interests of assuring that in the post–Cold War era, America and Europe remain essential partners in championing democracy, free markets, and human rights around the world."

— **Stuart Eizenstat**, Former U.S. Ambassador to the European Union, Under Secretary of Commerce, Under Secretary of State, and Deputy Secretary of the Treasury

"As a European-born, naturalized American, with a strong pragmatic business streak, Rock Schnabel brings a singular perspective to EU-U.S. relations. A must read for those who want to understand why this historic alliance is critical to global security and prosperity."

— **Niall FitzGerald**, Chairman, Reuters Ltd.

"GE knows that the regulations that American companies have to follow—even within America itself—are increasingly set in Brussels. Ambassador Schnabel explains why every global company must understand how the EU affects the way they do business. He also explains why, and how, the United States and Europe should work together for our mutual good. For business people, government policy makers, and other Americans wishing to understand the EU, this book is an indispensable guide."

— **Jeff Immelt**, Chairman and CEO, General Electric Company

"For Americans who have puzzled over the meaning of Europe's economic and political integration, and for those who have frankly wondered why they should care, Rock Schnabel's book is a revelation. In clear and forceful terms, our former ambassador to Brussels explains what the European Union is, how it works, and how it is changing the world balance of power."

— **Vernon E. Jordan Jr.**, Senior Managing Director,
Lazard Frères & Co. LLC

"The best book yet written on the geopolitical significance of the economic colossus of the European Union and its contentious relations with America. It is a must read for Europeans and Americans who are concerned about the future of the Atlantic partnership."

— **Robert Mundell**, Nobel laureate in Economics and "Father of the Euro"

"America's political and business leaders have long wondered, in Dr. Kissinger's famous phrase, whom they are supposed to call when they want to reach Europe. Ambassador Schnabel's book answers that question, and explains why the rise of the European Union is making transatlantic relations at once more challenging and potentially more fruitful for both sides."

— **Jorma Ollila**, Chairman and CEO, Nokia Corporation

"Ambassador Schnabel's well-written, intelligent and entertaining book should be read with profit by Americans and Europeans alike. Americans will learn what has been happening on this side of the Atlantic—some of it with American help. Europeans will discover what we look like to a smart insider and friend. All should recognize that America and Europe are best served when we work together as partners—the rest of the world is better off too."

— **Lord Patten of Barnes (Chris Patten)**, Chancellor,
the University of Oxford

"For more than half a century, the Atlantic Alliance has been the basis for European security and a cornerstone of global stability. Now Europe is beginning to develop a collective military identity of its own, without the participation of the United States. In this timely and insightful book, Ambassador Schnabel identifies the dangers and opportunities arising from the European Union's growing authority in security and defense; and explains why and how Europe and America should reaffirm our historic partnership."

— **General Joseph W. Ralston**, USAF (Ret.), Former Supreme
Allied Commander, Europe

The Next
Superpower?

The Next Superpower?

The Rise of Europe and Its Challenge to the United States

Ambassador Rockwell A. Schnabel

with Francis X. Rocca

ROWMAN & LITTLEFIELD PUBLISHERS, INC.
Lanham • Boulder • New York • Toronto • Oxford

ROWMAN & LITTLEFIELD PUBLISHERS, INC.

Published in the United States of America
by Rowman & Littlefield Publishers, Inc.
A wholly owned subsidiary of The Rowman & Littlefield Publishing
    Group, Inc.
4501 Forbes Boulevard, Suite 200, Lanham, Maryland 20706
www.rowmanlittlefield.com

www.thenextsuperpower.com

PO Box 317
Oxford
OX2 9RU, UK

Distributed by National Book Network

British Library Cataloguing in Publication Information Available

Library of Congress Cataloging-in-Publication Data

Schnabel, Rockwell A. (Rockwell Anthony), 1936-
    The next superpower? : the rise of Europe and its challenge to the
United States / Rockwell A. Schnabel, with Francis X. Rocca.
        p. cm.
    Includes bibliographical references and index.
    ISBN 0-7425-4547-4 (hbk : alk. paper)
    1. European Union. 2. European Union countries—Politics and
government—21st century. 3. United States—Foreign relations—
European Union countries. 4. European Union countries—Foreign
relations—United States. 5. World politics—21st century—
Forecasting. 6. International relations—Forecasting. I. Rocca, Francis X.,
    1963- II. Title.
JN30.S355 2005
940.56—dc33   2005012868

Printed in the United States of America

♾™ The paper used in this publication meets the minimum requirements
of American National Standard for Information Sciences—Permanence
of Paper for Printed Library Materials, ANSI/NISO Z39.48-1992.

Dedicated to

my children,

and to the memory of Marcel Xavier Rocca

Contents

Foreword

Congressman David Dreier

Chairman, Committee on Rules,
U.S. House of Representatives

WHEN I WAS first elected to Congress and came to Washington with Ronald Reagan in 1981, the European Union was nothing but an idea—one that seemed far-fetched. An EU predecessor, the European Economic Community, was the world's most important trading bloc after the United States, but few Americans (and not many more Europeans) ever expected that the ten countries of the EEC would ever achieve economic integration, let alone political unity, within our lifetimes.

The fall of the Berlin Wall and the collapse of the Soviet Union are the most significant European events of my time in public service, but a more quiet revolution has also been underway. It is part of a long process that dates back to before the start of the Cold War and has accelerated since the fall of the Soviet empire, yet one about which Americans remain virtually unaware.

European nations have formed a true single market in goods and labor and have removed many internal European barriers to trade in capital and services. Twelve nations have adopted the euro, giving up one of the most conspicuous instruments and symbols of national sovereignty in order to support a single European currency. The number of EU member states has swelled to twenty-five, including former members of the Soviet bloc—an unthinkable development two decades ago. And the Union may soon extend to the doorstep of the Middle East by allowing Turkey to accede to its membership. Meanwhile, EU institutions in Brussels have been granted increasing authority from national governments, not only in economic and trade policy but also in military and foreign policy (witness recent dealings and debates over the Middle East, Russia, and China).

Washington has, in turn, increased its respect for what is now a more cohesive and substantial transatlantic European partner than has ever previously existed. President Bush has continued his predecessors' practice of meeting with the heads of the EU at periodic summits, and in 2005 he made a historic visit to Brussels, where he reaffirmed America's commitment to further European integration and a strengthened transatlantic relationship.

On the front lines of that relationship stands the U.S. mission to the EU. For over three and a half years, during an intense period in transatlantic relations, my longtime friend and fellow Californian Rock Schnabel headed our mission. A European native, with previous diplomatic experience as the American envoy to Finland, an understanding of the Washington policy process acquired as Deputy Secretary of Commerce, and an appreciation of economic realities earned during a successful business career, no one was better qualified than Rock to represent U.S. interests in Europe.

Now he has drawn on the same qualities that make him such an effective advocate for his country in explaining the EU to Americans. This book, reflecting a rare combination of firsthand experience and long-range perspective, will enlighten anyone, American or otherwise, who wants to know more about an organization that will only increase in significance over the coming decades.

Introduction

Just before nine in the morning on a balmy, late-summer day in 2001, I walked into the headquarters of the Department of State in Washington, D.C., to report for my first day of work. Or to be precise, to report for a job that wasn't yet mine, since I still faced some rather important interviews on Capitol Hill. But a few weeks earlier, President George W. Bush had asked me to serve as the U.S. ambassador to the European Union, and I'd been happy and honored to accept.

The assignment would mean returning to public service after a decade in business, and moving back to the continent of my birth, to a city just two hours from the town where I'd grown up. I was curious to see how Europe had changed in a post–Cold War world, and eager to learn more about the unprecedented experiment of European integration, soon to extend for the first time beyond the former Iron Curtain. That morning, I would be starting preparations for the Senate hearings that I hoped would lead to my confirmation.

In the lobby of the State Department's main entrance on C Street, a young foreign service officer named Todd Huizinga, who'd been assigned to be my guide through the confirmation process, was waiting to meet me. Even before he said hello, I noticed his look of distraction and alarm.

"Something's happened in New York," Todd said. "A plane crashed into the World Trade Center."

We rode the elevator to the seventh floor, where the department's highest officials have their offices. In one of the mahogany-paneled conference rooms, dozens of staffers crowded around a large television. It took a few moments to understand, from the images being shown over and over on the screen, and from the words of the people around me, that in fact two planes had crashed, one into each tower. I remember thinking that somebody ought to *do* something, though I couldn't imagine what.

Then we heard the boom, as if an enormous tree branch had snapped and hit the ground just outside the building. Everyone went to the windows. Someone pointed out a widening stream of black smoke, rising from what would turn out to be the Pentagon.

I exchanged looks with several others, and saw that we were thinking more or less the same thing: that whatever had happened or was about to happen, the seventh floor of the State Department was probably not the best place for us to be. Todd and I agreed that the morning's business was now unlikely to stay on schedule. I took the stairs down and headed out of the building.

A large crowd had already formed on the sidewalk. Finding a bench in a small park nearby, I managed to reach my wife and children on my cell phone. Then the network was overwhelmed and no more calls got through. For the rest of the morning, I walked around town, trying to fathom the atrocity's human cost, and wondering how that morning's events would change the world.

My abortive first morning at State turned out to be a fitting introduction to my new job, because 9/11 would dramatically change the relationship between America and Europe, making it both more difficult and more necessary.

In the immediate aftermath of the attacks, the European reaction was deeply gratifying. On September 12, for the first time in history, NATO invoked the reciprocal defense clause (Article V) of its founding treaty, declaring the attack on America an attack on the entire alliance. On September 13, the French newspaper *Le Monde*, often critical of the U.S., ran its now-famous headline: *Nous sommes tous américains* ("We are all Americans"). One of the most moving gestures, to my mind, occurred on the open sea on September 14, when the German navy destroyer GFS *Lutjens* came alongside the destroyer USS *Winston Churchill*. The German ship was flying the American flag, and its crew, in dress uniform, stood at attention and held up a sign reading: "We Stand By You."

When I showed up in Brussels in early October, I was touched by the clearly heartfelt expressions of solidarity I received from European leaders and my fellow diplomats, even in the most formal contexts. On the first anniversary of 9/11, I was invited to address the European Parliament; and on the second anniversary, the assembled permanent representatives of the EU member states asked me to speak to them. In each case, it was the first time that such an honor had been extended to the American envoy.

British troops fought with the U.S. in Afghanistan in the fall of 2001, and several other EU countries sent peacekeeping forces there that winter. Yet even before the invasion of Afghanistan was complete, it was possible to hear European misgivings about American policy. Some suggested that, lacking Europe's long experience with domestic terrorism, we were overreacting to 9/11, even hysterically so. Others spoke with foreboding of Afghanistan as "another Vietnam."

Things grew worse over the course of 2002. As the U.S. headed toward a confrontation with Saddam Hussein, Europeans grumbled increasingly about America's supposed bellicosity. It was that summer that the prominent neoconservative writer Robert Kagan published an essay arguing that the EU and the U.S. held irreconcilable attitudes toward the use of military force: that "on major strategic and international questions today, Americans are from Mars and Europeans are from Venus."[1] Nor was Iraq the only source of conflict. Ongoing disputes over issues including the Kyoto Protocol on global warming, the International Criminal Court, U.S. tariffs on imported steel, and the international landmine ban greatly exacerbated transatlantic tension.

All of this came to a head that winter, when France and Germany led the opposition to America's Iraq policy in NATO and the UN Security Council. Demonstrators in the streets of European capitals carried signs comparing President Bush to Adolf Hitler, while few seemed to have a bad word for Saddam.

Many Americans took this personally. Our press and the Internet poured forth invective against "cheese-eating surrender monkeys." The French became fodder for the monologues of late-night talk show hosts. American wine drinkers organized a boycott of Bordeaux. On Capitol Hill, U.S. House cafeterias changed the name of the classic hamburger side dish to "Freedom Fries."

At least as great as the tensions between Europe and America in this period were those within the EU itself. In defiance of the Franco-German axis which had traditionally led the organization, the leaders of thirteen EU member states or soon-to-be member states—Britain, the Czech Republic, Denmark, Estonia, Hungary, Italy, Latvia, Lithuania, Poland, Portugal, Slovakia, Slovenia, and Spain—signed open letters backing the U.S. on Iraq.[2] All of these except for Slovenia later contributed troops to the American-led coalition there, as did founding EU member state the Netherlands. The eight post-Communist countries due to join the EU in May of 2004 were unanimous in supporting the American position, provoking France's President Jacques Chirac to declare that they were "not very well brought up" and had "missed an excellent opportunity to shut up." U.S. Secretary of Defense Donald Rumsfeld identified a split between what he called New and Old Europe, with the New pledging its loyalty to the United States.

Yet all this internal dissension occurred in the context of some momentous developments, less noticed in the United States, that showed the growing strength of European integration. On January 1, 2002, twelve countries from Ireland to Greece gave up their currencies and started using the euro. From the financial point of view, the occasion was merely symbolic, since the euro had already existed as a virtual currency for three years; but the near-flawless, continent-wide transition to the new money was an impressive display of the EU's competence. To ordinary citizens only vaguely aware of what the EU was, tangible coins and bank notes brought home the reality of integration.

At the same time as it introduced the euro, the EU prepared to receive its ten newest members, which finally joined the prosperous club in May 2004. As a result, a common body of law now extends from Ireland to the Russian border, and from the Arctic Circle to the eastern Mediterranean, an achievement without precedent in history.

I do not believe that most Americans appreciate the significance of these developments, nor of the half-century long process that led up to them, which has already turned Europe into an economic super-power and now promises to endow it with increasing geopolitical power as well. Though America was the original sponsor of European integration in the aftermath of World War II, most Americans have never paid much attention to the EU or its predecessor organizations. When it has shown up on our radar screen at all, we have tended to dismiss it as a trade organization, of interest only to economists or businessmen, or as a windy talk shop spouting forth inconsequential declarations in fancy country houses. As late as 1999, Henry A. Kissinger insisted that the euro would be a failure; and he had plenty of distinguished company.[3]

Not all Americans write the EU off, of course. Since the transatlantic controversy in the run-up to the Second Gulf War, America's euro-naysayers have been joined by an influential group of euro-doomsayers, who take European integration quite seriously—as a menace to the United States. In their view, popular among neoconservative political commentators, the EU is essentially a French-led, socialistic conspiracy to undermine U.S. power. A good example is a September 2003 cover story in *The Weekly Standard*, entitled "Against United Europe." The article, written by a British journalist, recommends an anti-EU strategy of cultivating ties with the Eastern member states and encouraging Britain not to adopt the euro, concluding: "It is not too late for the United States to help stop the European superstate from becoming a reality."

In fact, it is too late for the United States, or for Europe itself, to undo the reality of European integration. Despite recent turmoil over issues including the proposed EU constitution and the possible admission of Turkey, European nations have too much invested in the EU, and are too deeply intertwined with each other in economic, political, and legal ways, to split apart. In question is not the Union's survival but the form and direction that it will take, especially with regard to economic and foreign policy, in the coming years.

Nor is it in America's interest to undermine the EU project. The single European market is an economic boon to both sides of the Atlantic. An integrated Europe is a guarantee of stability among its members, and a force for democracy and Western values in the countries on its periphery, as seen most recently in the cases of Turkey and Ukraine. A strong EU is our natural partner in humanitarian efforts around the world. As the center of global power shifts toward China and India, promising to transform the international political and economic system in the next few decades, now is the time for the U.S. to work with a united Europe to secure the interests and defend the values of the West.

America should focus on engaging the EU all the more, at the level of the member states as well as of the supranational EU institutions, through dialogue and collaboration in that vast majority of areas where our views and interests coincide. Our goal should be to help manage the emergence of the EU as a global power, such that it remains committed to the Atlantic alliance which has ensured its security for over half a century, and to the free market policies that have made Europe and the U.S. the world's two richest economies.

Almost all European leaders understand that the EU's success, and even its very coherence, depend on a strong commercial and security relationship with America. A weaker transatlantic relationship means a weaker EU, and attempts to rally Europe around the banner of anti-Americanism will only divide it. Yet an opportunistic minority can exploit our disagreements to stir up mistrust of the U.S., whether merely for commercial gain or as part of a reckless geopolitical strategy positing Europe as a "counterweight" to America. The more closely we engage with Europe, the less opportunity there will be for such mischief.

I have written this book to explain what the EU is, why it matters, and how America can deal with it more effectively. In so doing, I have drawn on my background as a native European and naturalized American with experience in transatlantic commerce and diplomacy. For over three and a half years in Brussels, during an especially turbulent period in relations between the United States and Europe, I dealt extensively with EU policy makers and received thousands of visitors from Washington, hundreds of them at senior level, including President Bush in February 2005. I also visited all twenty-five EU member states, where I met hundreds of decision makers in government, business, and other fields. These encounters helped me to understand the complexity of our relationship, at once bilateral and multilateral, with European nations, and of those nations' relationships with each other inside the EU.

I hope that the following pages convey some of what I learned and thereby serve the goal of a stronger transatlantic relationship, a goal which I consider vital to the interests of both Europe and the United States.

Notes

1. Kagan, Robert, "Power and Weakness," *Policy Review*, 113, June/July, 2002. The essay was the basis for Kagan's book *Of Paradise and Power: America and Europe in the New World Order*, New York: Alfred A. Knopf, 2003.

2. Aznar, et al., "United We Stand," *The Wall Street Journal*, January 30, 2003, http://www.opinionjournal.com/extra/?id=110002994; "Statement of the Vilnius Group Countries in Response to the Presentation by the United States Secretary of State to the United Nations Security Council Concerning Iraq," February 5, 2003, http://www.useu.be/Categories/GlobalAffairs/Iraq/Feb0503VilniusIraq.html.

3. Reid, T. R., *The United States of Europe*, New York: Penguin, 2004, p. 5. Another example: In October 1994, a National Security Council staffer named Anthony Gardner contacted the office of then–Under Secretary of the Treasury Lawrence Summers to find out U.S. policy on the common European currency. He was told, "We don't need to have one," because the euro "is not going to happen."

Author's Note

SHORTLY BEFORE this book went to press, in the summer of 2005, French and Dutch voters rejected the constitutional treaty that the European Union's twenty-five member states had signed the previous fall, virtually ending chances for ratification of the constitution in its current form.

The long-term consequences are far from obvious. Some have foretold an end to the Union's geographic expansion, the dismantling of the common currency zone, and even disintegration of the EU itself.

As should be clear from the pages that follow, I believe that European nation-states have too great an interest in integration to give up on the organization they have spent over half a century building. With an aggregate gross domestic product practically equal to that of the United States, the EU gives this group of small- and medium-sized countries unsurpassed leverage over the global economy. And as a rising India and China shift the world's balance of geopolitical power, Europe's growing need to ensure its own security will call for more cooperation on the political level.

Yet as this book also explains, the EU has lately reached a crossroads, where it must choose between liberalizing its economy or pursuing the dirigiste policies that have held back growth in some of its largest members; and between enhancing its historic alliance with the United States or attempting to play the role of a geopolitical "counterweight" to America.

If this crisis over the constitutional treaty leads to an EU whose common economic policies are the product of free competition among the member states, and whose common foreign policies reflect Europe's predominantly Atlanticist orientation—an outcome I consider realistic, as long as European leaders show the necessary foresight and courage—it will not be the first time that the EU has seriously faltered before rebounding with heightened strength and ambition.

Summer 2005

The European Union

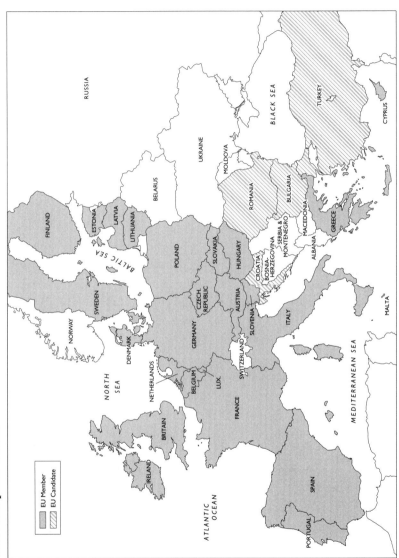

EU Member

EU Candidate

———⁓———

From the Old World to the New, and Back

MY STORY IS quintessentially American, yet it begins—and for this book's purposes ends—in Europe. Because my life has intersected at crucial points with the history of European integration, and because knowledge of my background helps explain the perspective from which I write, this chapter is a brief account of my life in the Old World and the New.

We Schnabels trace our roots to the city of Essen in western Germany, but since 1759 my branch of the family has lived in the Netherlands, where during the nineteenth century it prospered in the textile industry. At the turn of the twentieth century, my father grew up in affluent circumstances in the Hague, expecting that in due course he would go into his family business.

My father's plans were changed by the vicissitudes of international finance. Ironically, it was just when Germany's economy foundered in the early 1920s that my grandfather was forced to move back to his ancestral land, because of the crisis in the Weimar Republic. Most of my grandfather's capital was in German banks, and the German currency had become practically worthless beyond the country's borders. Not long after he arrived with his wife and children, the mark lost virtually all its value even within Germany. In the catastrophic hyperinflation of 1923, a single loaf of bread sold for 140 billion marks; and with coal and wood scarce, Germans burned bank notes by the stove-ful to keep warm. Several years later, when things had settled down, my grandfather took his family back to Holland.

No longer having a career laid out for him, and needing to make a living as soon as he became an adult, my father chose to become a journalist. He met and married a young woman, a classical pianist and singer by profession, from the southern part of Holland. They eventually had four children, of whom I was the third. Shortly after my birth in Amsterdam, we moved out to one of the suburbs.

Ours was a devout Roman Catholic family in a mostly Protestant society, and my father was always interested in religion. After he left journalism to go into the publishing business, religious and philo-sophical books were always prominent among his offerings. In the books he published, and in the way he lived, my father showed deep concern for the well-being of his fellow man. Under the influence of both Catholic social teaching and the civic ethos that is one of the noblest traits of Dutch society, my parents raised us with a strong sense of obligation to the community.

This sense of duty was put to the test by the ordeal that began in May 1940, when Germany invaded the Netherlands. Rather than follow orders to print Nazi propaganda, my father stopped publishing books altogether, and he continued to pay his Jewish employees against the orders of the Germans. This was, to say the least, asking for trouble, though I'm told that our German surname helped keep us out of the occupier's sights. But as the tide turned against the Third Reich, and its manufacturing industries grew increasingly short of labor, no able-bodied man in occupied territory was safe.

Because I was a toddler at the time, my memories of the period are sketchy. Yet I vividly recall soldiers marching up the driveway of our house, in the Amsterdam suburb of Heemstede, looking for my father. They were going to take him to Germany and put him to work in a factory, as they had already done to other men in our neighbor-hood. I can still see my mother standing at our front door, answering the soldiers in flawless German, telling them that my father had gone but she didn't know where.

It was true. My father stayed in hiding for a year, leaving us ignorant of his whereabouts for our own safety. My mother led the family in his absence. During the notorious "hunger winter" of 1944–1945, when the besieged Germans cut off the northern Netherlands from the liberated south, my mother traded jewelry for food to keep us alive.

Liberation came in May 1945, with the last of the Germans surrendering after five years of occupation. My father was home at last. We rejoiced in the survival of our immediate family, while mourning those who had not been so lucky, including some of our relatives.

Our elation at freedom regained soon wore off, and the hard work of rebuilding began. Feelings toward the vanquished foe remained bitter. For years after 1945, practically no one we knew bought anything made in Germany. My father, once he restarted the publishing business, never used another printing press from the land of Gutenberg. Had anyone told me at the end of the war that Germany and the Netherlands would soon start a voluntary process of economic unification, I would have taken it as an absurd joke.

This was when the United States first really entered my consciousness. There were U.S. troops everywhere, welcomed by all, and everyone knew that American money in the form of Marshall aid was stoking the recovery of Europe. It was easy to warm to America, not just because it had saved us from Hitler but because the Dutch were longtime Atlanticists. The Netherlands had been the second nation to recognize the sovereignty of the United States, in 1782; and as every Dutch schoolboy knew, our ancestors had founded America's greatest city under the name of New Amsterdam. After five years of Nazi censorship and propaganda, American movies and music fostered a surge of warm feelings for our cousins across the ocean.

Six decades later, listening to my fellow immigrant and Californian Arnold Schwarzenegger address the 2004 Republican Convention, I could recognize my own experience in the Governor's recollections of his Austrian childhood: "In school, when the teacher would talk about America, I would daydream about coming here. I would sit for hours watching American movies, transfixed by my heroes like John Wayne. Everything about America seemed so big to me, so open, so possible."

So when an invitation came from my mother's relatives in California to visit the land I knew from countless Hollywood movies, I accepted eagerly. The first leg of the trip was from Amsterdam to New York on a KLM Constellation, a four-engine prop plane. In the nearly five decades since, I have made that same trip hundreds of times, yet I still feel a twinge of the original thrill.

Southern California more than met my expectations. The sun, the sea, the relaxed yet dynamic style of life—all captivated me from the start. Yet the biggest attraction of all was the most surprising: Americans' admiration of ambition and success, so different from the envy and suspicion with which Europe has traditionally viewed high achievers.

To a young man brimming with energy and eager to kick off his career, this discovery was liberating. I felt as if I'd landed on a planet where the force of gravity was one-tenth what I was used to. By the end of my planned year, I knew I would be staying much longer.

America would not have seemed so instantly welcoming without the help of my hosts. The Kerckhoffs were a prominent family in Northern and Southern California, active in business and philanthropy. They took me into their house in San Marino; and once I had decided to stay in California, not only did they encourage my aspirations for a financial career, they actively helped me get my first job in the investment business.

There was, however, a major prerequisite to my settling down in America, once I had decided to do so: military service, which in those days was mandatory for all able-bodied young men. I enlisted in the California Air National Guard and was posted to a base just outside of Los Angeles, where I spent one weekend a month and two full weeks a year for the next six years. Those were years of peace for the United States, prior to our socially wrenching involvement in Vietnam, and my unit was never called to active duty.

The Guard allowed me to make some of my longest-lasting friendships and served as an intensive introductory course in American life and society. During this period I learned how to speak American English, as opposed to the British version I'd been taught.

It was also during my service that I met and married Marna Del Mar, a young woman from an old-line California pioneer family who had just started working as one of the first systems engineers at IBM. We eventually had two daughters, one son, and four grandchildren, all now living in Southern California, where all our children graduated from university.

Shortly after my wedding, I joined Bateman Eichler, a medium-sized brokerage house which later expanded into investment banking. I expanded my activities along with it, working my way up the ranks to president and a major owner. In 1983, eighteen years after I took my first job there, we sold the firm to what is now Wachovia Bank, and I concluded my first career. Over the following decade, I devoted myself almost exclusively to public service.

Since I'd already been involved in various community activities, it was natural for me to take part in the massive preparations for the 1984 Olympic Games in Los Angeles. Because of my background and continuing ties to the Netherlands, I was asked to serve as an envoy to the Dutch Olympic committee, the first time I would act as a link between my native continent and my adopted land.

In this period, I also started paying more attention to politics and government. I had joined the Republican Party shortly after becoming a U.S. citizen in 1965, essentially for the same reasons as Arnold Schwarzenegger: because the GOP was the party of individualism, limited government, low taxes, strong defense, and free enterprise. Though I'd helped raise funds for President Richard Nixon's reelection campaign in 1972, and for other Republican candidates later in the decade, I'd been too busy with work and family to get more involved.

Then in 1984, Holmes Tuttle, a California businessman and member of President Ronald Reagan's "kitchen cabinet," recruited me to work for Citizens for America, a national civic league dedicated to promoting the president's agenda. I had been a Reagan fan since his days as governor and was excited to take part, first in his reelection campaign and then in the administration's second term. My work with the Dutch Olympic committee had been so satisfying that I sought to represent my country abroad as an ambassador. Naturally I hoped for Holland but soon learned that this was not an option. The president proposed sending me to Finland, and I eagerly accepted.

Finland at the time I was there (1986–1989) occupied a peculiar place, at once marginal and central, in European geopolitics. Sharing a long common border with Russia, it observed a scrupulous neutrality, which allowed it to serve as a main economic and diplomatic conduit between the Soviet Union and the West. Because "Finlandization" was a synonym for geopolitical emasculation, I expected to find a people timorous and cowed, eager to do their powerful neighbor's bidding in exchange for a semblance of autonomy.

I should have realized that only the most resourceful and determined nation could have maintained a free, entrepreneurial economy and a democratic political system on the very edge of the Communist superpower. The Finns are in fact exceptionally independent—they were the only nation to pay off their World War I debts to the United States—but after centuries as Russia's neighbor and occasional foe, they are also deeply realistic. In their typically quiet way, they made clear to me how ardently they were rooting for America during what turned out to be the closing years of the Cold War. My most satisfying accomplishment as the U.S. ambassador to Finland was my part in negotiating a defense cooperation agreement between our governments before the fall of the Berlin Wall.

From my privileged vantage point in Helsinki, it became increasingly possible to foresee the end of the Cold War. Secretary of State George Schultz was a frequent visitor, sometimes passing through on his way to Moscow, sometimes meeting with his Soviet counterpart in the Finnish capital, as the two worked out arms reduction agreements. The high point of all this diplomatic traffic came in May 1988, with a three-day visit by President Reagan, en route to Moscow for his historic first visit and a meeting with General Secretary Mikhail Gorbachev. As I said goodbye to Reagan on the airport tarmac, knowing the momentous task he was going off to perform, I found myself too moved to deliver my prepared remarks.

I myself made several trips to Russia, where I got to know some of the key political figures of the time, including then–Foreign Minister Eduard Shevardnadze. But my most informative visit by far was one I made in a convoy of trucks from Helsinki to Moscow.

As a bit of background, which it is easy to forget in a post-Soviet world, the final thaw between the superpowers was also a period of high tension. We had no way of knowing that the Cold War would end virtually without bloodshed. On the contrary: it was all too easy to imagine that *glasnost* and *perestroika* would lead to dangerous instability, even to nuclear war. Driving stress levels all the higher were several diplomatic contretemps, among them the discovery that our brand new embassy in Moscow was riddled with electronic surveillance devices, including bugs imbedded in the very walls and foundations. Many of our diplomats were expelled on spurious charges of espionage.

In this climate of harassment, we in Helsinki took on the task of backing up our mission in Moscow. Because the Russians often made it hard to bring in supplies, we kept a warehouse stocked with everything from typewriters to cornflakes, which we would send over as necessary by truck. While it was easy for the Soviets to interfere with the movements of planes and trains, they could not keep out or look inside our trucks without transparently violating our prerogatives under international law. We ended up sending a number of trucks to Moscow every week. It became a major logistical effort, a miniature, terrestrial version of the Berlin airlift. On one occasion in 1987, I went along for the ride and was struck by the evidence of the Soviet empire's advanced decay: dilapidated buildings, roads, and infrastructure, and a police state clearly losing control, as people brazenly approached us to barter for our precious Western goods and currency.

As the Reagan administration drew to a close, I started planning my return to private life. Finland had been exhilarating, but my wife and I missed California. And though I had supported then–Vice President George H. W. Bush in his campaign for president, I did not expect to serve in his administration.

Then in January of 1989, while in Washington to attend President Bush's inauguration, I got an offer I couldn't refuse. Robert Mosbacher, the newly appointed Secretary of Commerce, asked me to serve as his number two.

Marna and I thought carefully. Washington was not L.A., of course, but we finally decided that it was close enough for her to practice her profession in California, and for us to keep in touch with our children there. For me, the job offered a stimulating challenge and the chance to reconnect to the business world.

While the Secretary of Commerce spends most of his time dealing with the outside world—representing the government to the business community, and communicating the interests of American business abroad—the Deputy Secretary handles internal operations. At the time, the department had more than 30,000 employees and an annual budget of over $3 billion. Until then, I had not managed a staff of more than 1,000.

Those were apprehensive times for American business, and for America in general. Even as the U.S. emerged as the world's sole superpower—the Berlin Wall came down in the Bush administration's first year—the U.S. economy was entering a recession, and self-doubt was widespread. With the eclipse of the Soviet threat, our unchallenged military dominance began to seem like a luxury that our economy could not afford. A widely discussed book in this period was *The Rise and Fall of the Great Powers* (1989) by the Yale University professor Paul Kennedy, who predicted that the U.S. was bound to follow its Spanish, French, and British predecessors in succumbing to the costs of "imperial overstretch."

The new economic champion, it was argued in dozens of bestselling books and countless articles, was the land of the rising sun. Those were the days when every business school student seemed to be studying Japanese, and major U.S. corporations were scrambling to adopt Japanese management techniques.

Focused as we were on Japan, few of us paid enough attention to some momentous economic changes taking place closer to home. The European Community (EC) was racing to create a true single market of twelve Western European states by 1992. The removal of almost all trade barriers between these countries—which included four of the world's largest economies: Germany, France, Britain, and Italy—would turn out to be a revolutionary event, permitting economies of scale and opportunities for market expansion comparable to those enjoyed by American industry.

We were not exactly oblivious to "1992." Secretary Mosbacher did go to Brussels to open a Commerce Department office that would deal directly with the increasingly powerful European Commission; and U.S. companies started hiring more lawyers and lobbyists to represent them there. But hardly any of us foresaw what it meant. Certainly I did not. Not only did the Europeans meet their deadline for single market reforms, but 1992 witnessed the launch of the single currency project that a decade later produced the euro. This was also the year that the EC changed its name to the European Union, signaling its members' intention to integrate politically as well as economically.

It was also an important year for me personally. Bob Mosbacher stepped down, and I took over his job as Acting Secretary. In that period I took part in the talks with Mexico and Canada that led to the North American Free Trade Agreement (NAFTA). That historic agreement, signed in the waning days of the first Bush administration and ratified under President Bill Clinton, brought to our own continent some of the same benefits that economic integration was bringing to Europe.

As the administration approached its end, I went back to L.A. and back into business. On the very day I resigned from Commerce, September 1, 1992, I joined with Robert C. McCormack, the former chief financial officer of the U.S. Navy and a past managing director of Morgan Stanley & Co., and Donald R. Dixon, also formerly of Morgan Stanley, to found Trident Capital Partners, a venture capital firm specializing in what would soon be known as the New Economy.

As it turned out, 1992 was the perfect moment to start investing in information technology. I wish I could say that this was due to my clairvoyance, but while my partners and I certainly foresaw big growth in the field, none of us imagined the coming bonanza.

Those were heady days. Practically overnight, people found that a small position they had acquired in a little start-up was worth many millions. It was hard to resist extravagant spending, and even harder to resist believing in your own financial genius.

As the oldest person on the Trident team, a group that was generally better educated and in some cases smarter than I was, my greatest contribution was reining in the others' enthusiasm. Experience teaches you skepticism and caution, and I knew the good times wouldn't roll forever. But by getting out at the right moments, we managed to ride out the downturns and build a solid reputation in the industry. (The firm has to date invested in some 100 companies.)

Toward the end of the Clinton years, I did what I could to help put a Republican back in the White House. I had met George W. Bush during his father's administration, and afterwards got to know him through a mutual friend, Brad Freeman. I was impressed by then-Governor Bush's leadership and determination, and when he announced his campaign for the presidency in 1998, I was among his original supporters.

A couple of months after President Bush took office in 2001, he asked me if I would serve in his administration. I was surprised when he finally proposed naming me the U.S. ambassador to the European Union. Although I had followed European events closely over the previous four decades, I was still trapped in an old way of thinking, according to which the EU was simply not as real as any of its constituent member states.

I asked the White House for time to think. And as I thought, read, and talked with knowledgeable people, I began to appreciate the revolutionary importance of the EU. Proud and powerful nations, bloody rivals for centuries, had freely given up large measures of sovereignty for the sake of peace and common prosperity. The result was a new sort of entity—neither a nation-state nor an international organization like the United Nations—that was already a formidable economic competitor with the U.S. and was promising to challenge our power in other ways as well. I could see that my background and experience on two continents had prepared me to deal with this entity on behalf of the United States.

So I went to Brussels, a mere 125 miles from my boyhood home, as a representative of my adoptive land. Over the next three and a half years, I was increasingly impressed by the skill and dedication of the men and women who make the EU work, in both the public and private sectors, not only at its center but also in the member states themselves, all twenty-five of which I visited during my tenure. No less impressive were the staff of the U.S. mission to the EU, their exceptional quality a sign of the growing importance that Washington was placing on Brussels.

On my first ambassadorial assignment a decade and a half earlier, I had watched from up close as the Soviet empire started to break up. Now I witnessed another revolution, as pieces of that defunct empire united peacefully with the West. And I discovered (in large part, rediscovered) what one writer has termed the "European Dream," a powerful vision of life distinct from—though not, I believe, incompatible with—the American Dream which I have lived.

————— ∼ —————

A Brief History of European Integration

THE EUROPEAN UNION today extends from the southern Mediterranean to hundreds of miles north of the Arctic Circle; and from the Atlantic shores of Ireland to the western frontiers of Russia and Turkey. Within these borders, 458 million people live under a common body of law, over 80,000 pages long and growing, that governs everything from quality standards for bananas to the definitions of an industrial monopoly.[1] Inside the bulk of this area, traveling between countries is as uneventful as driving from Pennsylvania to New Jersey, a freedom that will soon apply throughout the continental Union. Over 300 million EU citizens already share a common currency, and millions more are expected to do so in the next decade.

Europe has not been so united for 1,800 years, since the height of the Roman Empire. Yet unlike Rome, which was built through military conquest, this new European empire has been formed through the voluntary actions of democratically elected governments. Every country in the EU has actively sought to join it, often through strenuous effort. Other countries are doing likewise today.

In another sense, though, the EU does owe its existence to armed conflict, which provided a negative inspiration as well as the economic and political preconditions for European integration. After two world wars in three decades, Europeans climbed out of the rubble and resolved that such a thing would never happen again. They finally repudiated their ancient nationalisms for the sake of the common good, above all a lasting peace.

Or so goes what one diplomatic colleague of mine calls the "court history" of the EU, a narrative that stresses European idealism and self-determination as driving forces of the organization's growth. Yet for all the undeniable idealism behind it, the EU project has relied at every step on the pragmatism of national leaders, acting in the enlightened interest of their sovereign states. And while Europeans themselves are ultimately responsible for the EU's success, it is also appropriate—especially in light of recent transatlantic tensions—to recall that no country has backed European integration more forcefully or consistently than the United States.

From National Interests to the European Interest

World War II left Europe materially and spiritually devastated, with no obvious path to recovery. As Winston Churchill described the situation more than a year after Germany's surrender, "over wide areas a vast quivering mass of tormented, hungry, care-worn and bewildered human beings gape at the ruins of their cities and their homes, and scan the dark horizons for the approach of some new peril, tyranny or terror." Churchill's "sovereign remedy" for this plight, in the spirit of the recently founded United Nations, was to "re-create the European Family, or as much of it as we can, and to provide it with a structure under which it can dwell in peace, in safety and in freedom. We must build a kind of United States of Europe."

The United States of America also recognized the importance of European reconstruction, not only for humanitarian reasons, or merely because economic distress might lead to renewed conflict on the continent, but because political instability arising from economic chaos would favor the advance of Communism. Another of the U.S.'s key postwar aims was European integration, ideally in a political union of the Western states, to form a bulwark of stability and anti-Communism. The American-funded Marshall Plan was an important first step toward integration, since it required the participating nations to trade freely with each other and to adopt temporarily what was in effect a common currency. An essential element of the Plan was the reconstruction of Germany, Europe's once and future industrial powerhouse.

The continent did not rush to embrace these goals. France was leery of European integration as well as of German reconstruction. Only recently liberated from enemy rule, the French balked at ceding sovereignty to a supranational organization or exposing their industries to foreign competition. Nor was Paris inclined to rehabilitate Germany, which had invaded it three times in seventy years, and from which it demanded extensive reparations along with control of the highly industrialized Ruhr and Saar regions, as insurance against a resurgence of German militarism. Only the need for American aid persuaded France to lower its trade barriers and acquiesce in West Germany's participation in the Marshall Plan.

Yet it was from France that a solution to the Franco-German problem finally came, in the form of a proposal by Jean Monnet, a veteran diplomat and former businessman with strong ties to Britain and the United States. Monnet's proposal for a European Coal and Steel Community (ECSC), unveiled in 1950, meant putting production of those commodities under control of a supranational authority, an arrangement that would satisfy France's concerns with regard to the Ruhr and Saar.

Though Germany's industry had little to gain from the ECSC, its government supported the plan as a large step toward rejoining the company of respectable nations. The three small Benelux countries (Belgium, the Netherlands, and Luxembourg) saw economic advantages in joining, as well as a means of controlling their historically aggressive German neighbor. Italy, still largely agricultural, viewed the Community as a way to accelerate its industrialization and to wipe off the taint of fascism. Great Britain declined to join the other six, preferring to protect its coal and steel industries. For half a century thereafter, France and Germany together would decide the pace and direction of European integration.

In addition to reconciling former enemies, the ECSC was clearly intended as a safeguard against future wars, since coal and steel were at the time indispensable ingredients for manufacturing arms. Yet Monnet's plan was even more ambitious than that; he saw it as the first step toward a European superstate. As he wrote not long afterwards:

> Once nation-states and their leaders find themselves bound by rules, infringement of which will destroy common policies that are to their own advantage, these institutional bonds will serve not only to inhibit the occurrence of conflict, but also to mediate it if it does occur. Little by little this method of conducting policy in common will spread to all sectors of interstate relations until the members of the Community no longer deal with each other on a bilateral basis. At this point they will have become a federation just as the provinces of France were assembled in a national state at a moment favorable to this change in their status.[2]

Known today as the Monnet Method, this strategy of integration has been described as federalism by "stealth." With respect to its author, the suggestion of dishonesty is unfair, since Monnet made no secret of his federalist goals. But Monnet's approach to integration relies on what political theorists call "spill-over," whereby international cooperation in one policy area leads to cooperation in related areas, often technical fields apparently of interest only to bureaucrats. The result is that integration takes place below the radar of most political discourse, and in some cases even contrary to the long-range aims of national leaders.

The ECSC's success spawned further integration in the economic realm just three years later, when the same six nations pledged to abolish "obstacles to the free movement of goods, persons, services and capital" (thereafter known as the "Four Freedoms") in forming a common market.

Britain once again declined to take part, this time because the exclusive and interventionist character of a common market—as opposed to a free trade area—conflicted with its global commercial policies.[3] Only four years later, however, London would apply for membership in the European Economic Community (EEC), setting a lasting pattern of ambivalence toward European integration, with enthusiasm for commercial opportunities contending with suspicion of encroachments on national sovereignty.

As with the ECSC, so too with the EEC the six founding members were motivated above all by national interests. German leaders were anxious to reconcile with their neighbors, who were at least as anxious to lock the resurgent industrial power in a structure that would make its future aggression impractical if not unthinkable. Italy needed an outlet for its surplus of unskilled labor. French agriculture needed an external market, and as the government had come to see, French industry needed outside competition to make it modern and efficient.

Though Paris's most obvious incentives for joining the EEC were economic, it also discovered a political interest. In 1958, General Charles de Gaulle was elected president of France for the second time.[4] Seeking to restore his country to greatness, de Gaulle saw the EEC as a vehicle through which it could play a global role commensurate with its heritage. That meant France acting as the organization's political leader, a position to which the still-penitent Germany could make no pretensions. De Gaulle accordingly blocked the admission of Britain until his retirement in 1969, rather than share influence with a nation with its own claims to be a world power.

De Gaulle's strategy also required that France not cede any of its sovereignty to the EEC itself. The president's ideal of integration was what he called a *Europe des patries* ("Europe of nations"), in which countries would cooperate along the lines of intergovernmental organizations such as NATO or the UN Security Council, where binding decisions require unanimity, effectively giving every member a veto.

Yet it was precisely this feature that Monnet had blamed for the League of Nations' failure. Decisions in the EEC, as in the ECSC before it, were to be made by a "qualified majority" (as distinct from a simple majority) of member states, meaning that a national government could be required to follow a policy against its wishes. This was the essence of the federation that Monnet envisioned for Europe. To de Gaulle, it was intolerable. The conflict came to a head in 1965, when France withdrew from EEC proceedings and brought the organization to a halt for six months. For two decades thereafter, every member state would hold a veto on all significant decisions.

Now that the organization was practically incapable of thwarting the will of national governments, membership in the European Community (as it was known after 1967) became a more inviting proposition to countries traditionally jealous of their sovereignty, including Britain, Ireland, and Denmark, which joined in 1973. But the organization they joined was an increasingly ineffectual one.

One sense in which the EC nonetheless remained relevant was as a sort of certification body for modern European states, attesting that they met prevailing standards of political and economic freedom. In the late 1970s and early 1980s, the EC helped guide the former right-wing dictatorships of Greece, Portugal, and Spain in their transitions to democracy, by setting the terms of their accession to the Community. The EU played the same role on an even larger scale two decades later, with the admission of post-Communist states in Central and Eastern Europe, and continues to play it even today, as aspiring member Turkey enacts dramatic legal and political reforms in accordance with criteria set in Brussels.[5]

Yet the EC would never have recovered the dynamism of its early days without active leadership. It found that leadership in Jacques Delors, president of the European Commission from 1985 to 1995. The Commission (whose structure, powers, and duties, along with those of the other major EU institutions, are described in appendix A) is dedicated to the general European interest, and has traditionally been the powerhouse of integration. Delors spent his decade in office increasing the powers of the supranational Community institutions, and extending the areas of pan-European cooperation.

In this task Delors found an unlikely ally in British Prime Minister Margaret Thatcher. I say unlikely, not just because Thatcher was a strong believer in the free market, whereas Delors was a Socialist, but because she was as fierce a defender of national sovereignty as de Gaulle had been. At a meeting with leaders of the other member states in 1979, shortly after her election as prime minister, Thatcher complained about her country's disproportionate contribution to the

EC's budget and memorably demanded "our money back." She eventually obtained an annual rebate which continues to this day.

Thatcher and Delors were nevertheless of one mind on the need to realize the unfulfilled promise of a common market, by eliminating trade barriers such as border controls, differences in product standards, and varying rates of excise and sales tax. London therefore backed the plan, drawn up by a British member of the Commission in 1985, to form a "single large market by 1992."

The ambitious, and largely successful, effort that ensued was decisive for the EC in more than economic terms. It transformed the organization's internal political dynamic. In order to pass the hundreds of laws necessary in such a short time, argued the Commission, it was necessary to return to qualified majority voting. The result was a loss of the national veto in almost all areas to do with the single market. A precedent had been set. Qualified majority voting has since then been gradually extended to other policy areas, and the trend shows every sign of continuing.

Delors's presidency also produced the agreement that would lead to the single most powerful instrument and symbol of European integration, the common currency. Supporters of monetary union saw this as following logically from the existence of a single market, but to Thatcher, the "single currency [was] about the politics of a federal Europe by the back door." Her resistance provoked controversy in her own party, and contributed to her downfall in 1990.

Wider versus Deeper?

As the EC worked to liberalize internal trade by the self-imposed deadline of 1992, the world just beyond its borders was changing in a far more radical way, with the crumbling of the Soviet empire. The most obvious implication of this event for the EC was the potential reunification of Germany.

When the Berlin Wall fell in November 1989, the population of West Germany was 61 million, only slightly larger than the populations of France (56 million), Britain (57 million), or Italy (57.6 million). But East Germany had another 16.6 million people. Merging the two Germanys would produce by far the largest EC member state, and raise the prospect of Germany playing a political role commensurate with its economic dominance.

For the U.S., a stronger Germany would mean a more effective partner in the post–Cold War international system, and Washington accordingly offered crucial encouragement for reunification. But many European leaders, including Britain's Thatcher, found the same prospect alarming. The idea was particularly disturbing for France, which had always seen itself as the senior half of the Franco-German partnership. A month after the fall of the Berlin Wall, in December 1989, President François Mitterrand traveled to Kiev, where he joined Soviet President Gorbachev in reaffirming support for an "East German identity" and warning against precipitous border changes. The French President traveled that same month to East Berlin, in an apparent sign of support for the Communist regime.

Mitterrand soon resigned himself to a united Germany, but only after obtaining West German Chancellor Helmut Kohl's promise to participate in the common currency. The euro (as it was later named) would not only enhance France's economic power, but rein in that of its rich and populous German neighbor. Kohl was willing to surrender the strong deutsche mark, fruit and symbol of Germany's postwar economic triumph, to reassure the rest of Europe that his country remained committed to the continent's unity.

The German question was only the first major challenge that the end of the Soviet empire posed for the EC. With the fall of the Iron Curtain, the organization's enlargement to the East suddenly became more than a theoretical possibility. Absorbing Austria, Finland, and Sweden, whose neutrality had kept them out during the Cold War, was relatively easy, since these countries were all wealthy and solidly democratic. Far more problematic were the post-Communist states, whose economic development and political cultures were stunted by decades of totalitarianism, but which were eager to join the West.

Germany was quickly rebuilding commercial ties to match its long-standing cultural bonds with the Central and Eastern European countries, and supported their admission to the Community. France on the other hand had serious reservations. The accession of heavily agricultural Poland would strain the lavish system of subsidies (the Common Agricultural Policy) from which French farmers had profited since the late 1950s. More generally, the proliferation of EC member states would make it harder for France to play its traditional leadership role in the organization. After all, the post-Communist states had only recently regained their sovereignty, and would be in no rush to take orders from Paris. Other EU member states also viewed enlargement with concern. The poorer Mediterranean countries, especially Spain, did not welcome an influx of needy members with which to compete for the Community's so-called structural or cohesion funds.

Meanwhile, the United States bolstered the candidacies of the Central and Eastern states by bringing them into NATO, despite French and German fears that this would antagonize Russia. Since 1989, the U.S. has given over $7.1 billion, under the Support for East European Democracy (SEED) Act, to assist in the development of market economies and pluralistic societies in post-Communist lands, with a stated aim of helping those nations to qualify for EU membership.

The decisive factor in favor of enlargement was finally moral: the force of Western Europe's avowed principles of unity, freedom, and cooperation. Blocking the entry of newly liberated states would have confirmed the harshest caricatures of the Community as a protectionist "rich man's club" instead of a genuine effort to bring lasting peace and prosperity to the continent. Faced with such a threat to the legitimacy of integration, Western European leaders were forced to live up to their ideals.

As the member states debated enlargement through the 1990s, they expanded the areas in which they acted in common. The EC nations agreed to monetary union in 1992, surrendering a key element of sovereignty—the right of a nation's central bank to set its own interest rates—as well as the symbolic power of coins and banknotes bearing emblems of national identity. In the long run, a common currency would also raise pressure for common economic policies and tax rates.

The same agreement that established monetary union (the Maastricht treaty) introduced a new name: the European Union (EU), bearing stronger supranational connotations than the various versions of "Community" which had until then identified the integra-tion project.

Also beginning with Maastricht, the purview of EU institutions was extended to foreign policy, defense, and "justice and home affairs" (including immigration and what we now call homeland security), all previously exclusive domains of the member states. Because these areas were so politically sensitive, every nation was given a veto on any common action. But since the late 1990s, some justice and home affairs legislation—notably in the area of border security—has become subject to qualified majority voting, with the member states handing increasing administrative powers to the Commission in Brussels.

There is an undeniable logic to this trend, the logic of the Monnet Method. If a single market requires the free movement of persons among EU member states, this in effect creates common bor-ders. Once an immigrant, legal or otherwise, makes it into Italy, he can travel all the way to Sweden without showing his passport at a single border crossing. Such a situation naturally calls for common policies on border control, refugee status, and the repatriation of ille-gal aliens.

Here is "spill-over" on a grand scale. And the same phenome-non occurs in less predictable ways. Without the EU member states planning it, responsibility for certain policy areas can pass over to Brussels, just because a related area is already under the Commission's jurisdiction. For example, when the U.S. negotiated our 2004 agree-ment with the EU on the Galileo satellite navigation system, a mat-ter with serious implications for American military capabilities, the principal negotiating parties across the table from us were not repre-sentatives of the various European nation-states, as had always been the case with defense-related treaties, but officials of the European Commission. Decisions on defense matters are supposed to be the prerogative of the member states, but under the EU system, satellite navigation is essentially about transportation, which along with other issues pertinent to the single market, now falls under supranational control.

Integration in this way—by a kind of bureaucratic momentum—might seem to suggest that the road to European federation can bypass the messiness of electoral politics. But as the EU has grown to a size that ordinary citizens can no longer ignore, many have expressed reservations about the whole project. Danish voters rejected the Maastricht Treaty in a 1992 referendum, and approved it only narrowly when asked to reconsider. A referendum on the same treaty in France passed by a majority of only 51.05 percent. Ireland had to hold two referenda in 2001 before its citizens approved the Nice Treaty, preparing the way for admission of the Central and Eastern states. And in Britain, an explicitly anti-EU party won 17 percent of the vote in the 2004 elections to the European Parliament.

Long a merely consultative body without real authority, Parliament has since the 1990s acquired effective veto power in an increasing number of areas of EU law (though it still cannot initiate legislation). This enhancement of Parliament is a response to the so-called "democratic deficit"—that is, the EU's domination by unelected supranational bureaucrats in Brussels and national politicians who meet at closed-door intergovernmental summits. But consistently falling rates of voter participation in Parliamentary elections, to 45.7 percent in 2004 from 63 percent in 1979, hardly suggest that citizens are taking the institution more seriously.[6]

The most impressive display to date of popular dissatisfaction with the EU came in late spring of 2005, when the citizens of France and the Netherlands, two of the six founding member states, voted to reject the constitutional treaty that their governments had signed the previous year.[7] In my view, the EU is increasingly paying the price for its stealthy success of earlier decades, for integrating at the administrative level without offering the public a clear vision of integration and its benefits. National leaders have not helped matters by repeatedly laying the blame on Brussels for unpopular yet necessary economic reforms.

One factor in the French and Dutch rejections of the constitutional treaty was apparently anxiety over the EU's 2004 enlargement, which brought in eight Central and Eastern states—the Czech Republic, Estonia, Hungary, Latvia, Lithuania, Poland, Slovakia, and Slovenia—along with the two Mediterranean island nations of

Cyprus and Malta. Many warned that making the EU so economically and culturally heterogeneous would reduce the organization's capacity to act; that a "wider" Union would come at the expense of "deeper" integration. Public opinion surveys conducted for the European Commission in the two years preceding enlargement showed rising numbers of people in both old and new member states who identified exclusively with their nationalities rather than with Europe as a whole.[8]

"After World War II there was such a strong feeling in Western Europe that we should prevent war, that there was such a strong sense of collaboration, but now people wonder why they should send tax money to a village in Estonia," a diplomat from one of the founding member states has told me, wondering whether such a far-flung group "will feel parts of the same community and feel sufficient solidarity to be willing to go for a common future."

As a result of the growing divergence among the member states, the likelihood has increased of a "multi-speed" EU, in which subgroups of member states will move ahead of the others with integration in certain areas of law and policy. This is already the case with the euro, which Britain, Denmark, and Sweden have declined to adopt as their currency; with the Schengen Agreement on cross-border travel, which Britain and Ireland have chosen not to sign (EU citizens still have to show their papers when they enter those countries); and with aspects of common defense and security policy (see chapter 4), whereby a still-undetermined number of states will combine to form the beginnings of a European army. Whether these and other such initiatives eventually draw the other member states into participating, or whether they turn the EU into a conglomerate of larger and smaller intergovernmental organizations—a far cry from the federalist vision of Jean Monnet—will be a central question over the coming decade.

In one respect, at least, the new member states have undoubtedly changed the EU, by ending Franco-German hegemony within it. Efforts by Paris and Berlin to rally Europe against America's Iraq policy were, among other things, an attempt to reassert their leadership of the EU on the eve of its enlargement. The attempt failed most clearly with the post-Communist countries, who even before they had officially joined the EU, went out of their way to declare their support for the American position. France's President Jacques Chirac did little to enhance his influence by calling these declarations "infantile" and "dangerous," and saying that the accession states had "acted frivolously" and were "not well brought up," having "missed a great opportunity to shut up." French rejection of the constitution, driven largely by fear of low-wage competition from so-called "Polish plumbers," has only further reduced Paris's influence over an enlarged EU.

Although a break with long tradition, the weakening of Franco-German leadership is in another sense true to the EU's fundamental dynamic. Nations belong to the EU in order to serve their interests. It is the constant balancing and mediation of national interests that permit the organization to survive and grow. As Viscount Etienne Davignon, a former vice president of the Commission and longtime observer of European institutions, put it to me: "There is no dominant power in the EU, though some countries are more or less influential. You see this every day. Whenever two or three countries try to dominate they fail. . . . There are no constant majority or minority alliances; the compositions are always changing according to the agenda. That's one reason the EU has continued to work, because there is no permanent majority and no permanent minority that never gets its say."

The main agenda of European integration for its first half century was economic growth, the containment of Germany, and the preservation of peace among European nations, as well as between the superpowers. Over the generation to come, the EU's major aims will include maintaining competitiveness in a global economy, defining stable borders with Russia and the Middle East, and projecting European power in the world. To succeed at these goals will demand ever more compromise between national and supranational interests. The EU must increasingly act as more than the sum of its parts, and this in turn will require European citizens and their leaders to identify with the Union as a whole as well as with their home countries. Beyond the complex economic and geopolitical forces with which the EU must contend, it faces no greater challenge than this need for a common identity.

Notes

Among the general sources I have drawn on for this chapter are Torbiörn, Kjell M., *Destination Europe: The Political and Economic Growth of a Continent*, Manchester and New York: Manchester University Press, 2003; and Dedman, Martin J., *The Origins and Development of the European Union, 1945–95: A History of European Integration*, London and New York: Routledge, 1996.

1. The entire body of European Union law, including treaties among the member states, regulations and directives passed by the EU institutions, and decisions of the EU courts, is known as the *acquis communautaire*. The Eur-Lex website provides a single point of entry for online versions of all EU legal texts: http://europa.eu.int/eur-lex/en/index.html.

2. Anonymous, "What Jean Monnet Wrought," *Foreign Affairs*, April 1977.

3. For more on this subject, see chapter 3.

4. De Gaulle had headed France's postliberation provisional government from 1944 to 1946, before withdrawing from politics.

5. The three broad requirements of membership, known as the Copenhagen Criteria (after the city where they were promulgated in 1993), are (1) "stability of institutions guaranteeing democracy, the rule of law, human rights and respect for and protection of minorities"; (2) "the existence of a functioning market economy as well as the capacity to cope with competitive pressure and market forces within the Union"; and (3) "the ability to take on the obligations of membership including adherence to the aims of political, economic & monetary union." Candidate countries must also bring their laws into conformity with all EU legislation, the *acquis communautaire*. Source: the European Commission's website, http://europa.eu.int/comm/enlargement/intro/criteria.htm.

6. Source: website of the European Parliament, http://www.elections2004.eu.int/ep-election/sites/en/results1306/turnout_ep/turnout_table.html.

7. The full text of the constitution can be found at http:///europa.eu.int/constitution/constitution_en.htm.

8. *Eurobarometer Spring 2004: Public Opinion in the European Union*, Joint Full Report of Eurobarometer 61 and CC Eurobarometer 2004.1, The European Commission: Brussels, 2004, p. B.95. http://europa.eu.int/comm/public_opinion/archives/eb/eb61/eb61_en.pdf.

CHAPTER

THREE

The European Union as
an Economic Superpower

A SUPERPOWER, ACCORDING to the Oxford English Dictionary, is a state "which has the power to act decisively in pursuit of interests which embrace the whole world." By that definition, the European Union qualifies as a superpower on economic grounds alone.

Ask Jack Welch. In 2001, the then-CEO of General Electric saw his plans for a merger with Honeywell International dashed by the European Commission. Never mind that both companies were American and that the $42-billion deal had been approved by Washington. The Commission forbade the merger, claiming that the resulting company would have held back competition in the international aerospace industry.

Or ask Bill Gates. In 2004, despite Microsoft's previous settlement with the U.S. Department of Justice, Brussels ordered the software titan to pay a €497-million fine for antitrust violations, share proprietary information with competitors, and offer customers an alternative version of its Windows operating system. While the order applied to European sales only, the Commission made it clear that it *could* force Microsoft to change its practices worldwide—and warned that it might do so in the future.

Or ask the farmers, from Indiana to Namibia, who have stopped planting high-yield biotech crops for fear of losing access to the

European market. The EU's de facto ban has slashed American corn exports to Europe by more than 90 percent and cost the U.S. soy industry an estimated $1.6 billion—all without any scientific evidence that such crops are anything but safe. The government of famine-stricken Zambia turned down donations of biotech corn lest they jeopardize the country's exports to Europe. In 2004, the U.S.-based Monsanto Company abandoned plans to sell the world's first biotech wheat for the same reason.

Finally, ask Ronald McDonald. After the Commission ruled that the chemicals used in soft plastic toys were unsafe for children, McDonald's stopped including such toys with Happy Meals, even at its U.S. restaurants.

As these people and many others can tell you, the EU is increasingly seeking to act as the world's economic regulator. It is a plausible candidate for this role because the integration of twenty-five national economies has formed the largest single market in the developed world: 458 million consumers, more than the U.S and Japan together. A market that big is also why the Commission could credibly threaten to use trade sanctions to influence the 2004 U.S. presidential election.[1]

The EU today has the second largest economy in the world, with an aggregate gross domestic product of $11.65 trillion in 2004, compared with $11.75 trillion for the United States (in terms of purchasing power parity). European corporations such as Nokia, Vodafone, and Daimler-Chrysler are global leaders in their industries; and in 2005, the multinational EU aerospace conglomerate Airbus was expected to sell more passenger jets than America's Boeing for the third straight year. Though Europe's growth has lagged in recent years, changes underway promise to make its economy only more powerful. Competitive pressures within the EU's single market, and especially within the "euro zone" of twelve nations using the common currency, are driving companies to restructure and grow more efficient, and raising the heat on governments to deregulate, cut taxes, and take other liberalizing measures. The euro makes it easier to compare economic results across borders, another spur to reform. The accession of ten mostly post-Communist countries in 2004 has introduced a highly educated, low-cost workforce and a class of young, ambitious entrepreneurs. These new member states have high growth rates and low-tax, pro-business policies that were provoking reforms in older members even before enlargement. Completion of the EU's single market in financial services will make capital markets deeper and more liquid, lowering the cost of capital and facilitating entre-preneurship across the continent. Single markets in services, energy, and transportation, also in the works, will likewise boost growth.

Most of these changes have been and will continue to be painful and slow, and therefore politically controversial, but the medium- to long-term effects will be deeply invigorating. And don't forget Europe's strong fundamentals. Compared with the U.S., the major EU economies have low current-account deficits, low consumer debt, and high savings rates, representing pent-up demand that should fuel growth once confidence increases. Whereas America's high deficits and low savings rate are setting us up for a jolt when the bill for our consumption, financed with foreign money, finally comes due—a dan-ger made far more urgent by the emergence of the euro as an alterna-tive global reserve currency.

For at least the next decade and probably two, the EU will be the only world economy on par with America. In Japan, an "iron triangle" of big business, political parties, and government bureaucracy contin-ues to block the structural reforms necessary to end stagnation. India and China, though well are on their way to becoming strong com-petitors to the U.S., are today still heavily agricultural nations in the throes of industrialization. China's GDP could be as large as America's by the year 2020, but even if its economy grows three times as fast as ours, China's *per capita* income will not match that of the U.S. until the second half of the twenty-first century.[2] Explosive growth has severely stressed China's immature financial system, and the country remains (lest we forget) under the political and economic control of the Communist Party, with all the inefficiency and corruption that entails. Twentieth-century history has taught us that a nation cannot grow truly rich without a free economy and the rule of law, and China must acquire these before it can catch up with the U.S. or the EU.

The rise of Europe, our largest trade and investment partner, ought to be great news for America. U.S. companies make half their global earnings in the EU, over $77 billion in 2003. European companies employ over 4 million people in the U.S., and European investors are indirectly responsible for millions more American jobs. The importance of European business to the U.S. economy is largely hidden behind brands that most American consumers do not consider foreign. How many in the U.S. realize that Shell and Unilever are Anglo-Dutch concerns, or that the French hotel group Accor owns Red Roof Inns? Europe is also a "key supplier of capital or liquidity for the debt-stretched United States."[3] Growth in the $2.5-trillion-a-year transatlantic commercial relationship would thus mean more revenue for our corporations, more capital for our entrepreneurs, more opportunities for our investors, and more jobs for our workers.

A strong partnership between the U.S. and the EU, which together account for more than 40 percent of the world's GDP and over a third of world trade, is vital to the prosperity of the globe. Not only can it determine the success of international trade negotiations, but commercial relations help sustain transatlantic collaboration in other areas, including counterterrorism, defense of human rights, environmental protection, hunger relief, and disease control.

Nevertheless, America has reason to fear a richer and more unified EU. With a regulatory regime that it seeks to impose on the rest of the world, it could stifle the freedom of U.S. business to innovate and grow. Just as the EU-mandated GSM wireless standard, subsequently adopted in much of Asia, stunted international sales of American-made mobile phones in the late 1990s, other common industrial standards could serve as global barriers to U.S. products, ranging from satellite-based navigational devices to boilers. Brussels's efforts to manage global competition through antitrust regulation could lead to higher prices and fewer choices for U.S. consumers. The euro could even dethrone the dollar as the preferred global reserve currency, threatening our ability to pay for energy and military defense.

Whether the EU continues to be our greatest commercial partner or turns into our most formidable economic rival depends on a choice that Europe is now in the process of making, between two distinct schools of economic policy. One alternative follows in the French tradition of state planning and intervention. The other lies closer to the Anglo-American model of free-market capitalism. These two approaches have contended for primacy throughout the history of European integration. Now, as the EU nears its geographic limits and its maturity as a political organization, this choice will define the sort of economic regime it is to be. It is a decision of enormous consequence not only for Europe, but also for America and the rest of the world.

Liberal versus Dirigiste

The EU is at heart a political project, but at its start and for decades thereafter, its scope was almost exclusively economic. Its founders were European statesmen seeking, in the aftermath of World War II, to build an international system that could prevent a repeat of the strife that had devastated their continent. These statesmen offered ambitious proposals, enthusiastically endorsed by the U.S., for joining the nations of Western Europe in military and political union. But national governments, jealous of their sovereignty, refused.

Economic integration proved more appealing. France and Germany, Europe's two biggest economies, had complementary interests in such an arrangement: France needed a market for its large farming sector, while Germany sought customers for its industrial exports. The two countries agreed to a common market with Italy and the Benelux states (Belgium, the Netherlands, and Luxembourg), first in coal and steel, then in labor, goods, services, and capital.

It is significant that Great Britain, the largest European economy at the end of World War II, was absent at the creation of the common market. After all, Churchill himself called for a "United States of Europe" in 1946, and the British government proposed a free trade area with the continental states in the 1950s.[4] But the common market was no mere free trade area, such as the U.S would later form with Canada and Mexico in the North American Free Trade Agreement (NAFTA)—that is, a group of states that simply agree to lift tariffs and other trade barriers between them. Nor was it only a larger-scale version of the Zollverein, the nineteenth-century customs union that formed the basis for the modern German state (though the Zollverein was an important model and inspiration for the EU). The European common market was a far more complicated invention, designed according to economic principles that Britain's leaders viewed as foreign to their values and contrary to their interests.

Dirigisme is a relatively new word for a French tradition at least three and a half centuries old. Jean-Baptiste Colbert, finance minister to Louis XIV, carried out an ambitious plan to build up France's industries through tariffs, state investment, and precise standards for manufactured goods. Napoleon reinforced the French practice of central planning and state intervention. Colbert's spiritual descendants are the government planners, graduates of elite schools such as the École Nationale d'Administration, who dominate French economic life to this day.

In opposition to the dirigiste school stands that of free-market capitalism, most famously expounded by the Scottish economist Adam Smith in *The Wealth of Nations* (1776). Europeans use the word "liberalism" (which of course means something very different in America) to refer to this economic philosophy, which relies on what Smith called the "invisible hand" of the market to decide the best distribution of resources in the global economy. Because it has long characterized the policies of Britain, and more recently of the U.S., it is often described as "Anglo-Saxon" or "Anglo-American," as opposed to "Continental," economics. The crucial difference between the schools is the degree to which they place their trust in state planning and intervention on the one hand or free-market forces on the other.

The major architects of European economic integration have been French technocrats of the dirigiste type. Jean Monnet, who proposed and ran the earliest version of what would become the EU, also planned and directed France's postwar economic recovery, marked by heavy public spending on industry and agriculture. Monnet's protégé, Pierre Uri, drafted the Treaty of Rome (1957), which established the common market. Jacques Delors, who as President of the European Commission from 1985 to 1995 oversaw the extension of the common market and planned the common currency, is a French Socialist and former economics and finance minister.

The Treaty of Rome clearly betrays its dirigiste authorship, calling for a common external tariff on imports from outside the community of six countries and the "approximation of the laws of Member

States to the extent required for the functioning of the common market."[5] The latter idea has often been described as "leveling the playing field." Germany, for instance, had to shorten its work week and guarantee longer vacations in accordance with French practice, lest its more business-friendly policies give German companies an "unfair" edge on their competitors across the Rhine. To prevent "distortions" of competition, member state governments coordinated their subsidies to national industries.[6]

Most elaborate of the leveling measures was the Common Agricultural Policy (CAP), a system of subsidies, tariffs, and guaranteed prices designed to protect Europe's—and especially France's—farmers. It remains the most expensive EU project, eating up about 40 percent of the union's €100-billion budget (twice what the U.S. spends on agricultural subsidies), and is a major reason why Europeans spend much more of their income on food than Americans do. Because its subsidies were until recently all tied to production, the CAP has been responsible for vast surpluses, famously described as "butter mountains" and "wine lakes." Dumping these products on the external market at artificially low prices deals a heavy blow to developing economies, which also suffer from their restricted access to the European market. According to the relief agency Oxfam, the EU's sugar policy alone has cost Mozambique more than one-third of what it has received in EU development aid.[7]

The common market unquestionably brought growth to postwar Europe, most dramatically in the case of underdeveloped Italy, whose "economic miracle" of industrialization in the 1950s and 1960s would have been impossible without access to Northern European markets. German competition stimulated the modernization of French industry. But reality fell far short of the promise in the Treaty of Rome. Although the member states no longer blocked each other's goods with tariffs or quotas, they set up a host of nontariff barriers, such as national product standards, national preferences for public contracts, and heavy paperwork for truck drivers crossing national borders.

Not until the mid-1980s did the next push for integration come. By that time the EU (then called the European Community) had twelve member states, including Britain, which had finally joined in 1973. British Prime Minister Margaret Thatcher, a zealous advocate of free markets, gave crucial support to Jacques Delors in his drive to complete what was thereafter known as the "single market."

Two decades later, it is clear that the EU's single market has been in many respects a liberalizing project. Thanks to the removal of trade barriers and the privatization of government monopolies, Europeans have seen their phone bills plummet and have grown used to jetting across the continent for less than the price of a bus ticket. Inefficient and overstaffed companies have restructured or gone out of business, and the resulting growth has more than compensated for their loss. The Commission estimates that the single market has created more than 2.5 million jobs since 1993.

All of this may seem to mean victory for Anglo-American liberalism. But there is one all-important respect in which the single market hews much closer to the dirigiste approach than to that of the free traders: regulation.

We can see both liberalism and dirigisme at work in the EU's competition (i.e., antitrust) policy. The competition authority has struggled tirelessly, though not always successfully, to stop member state governments from propping up foundering "national champions," such as the French engineering group Alstom or the Italian airline Alitalia. This unpopular task, which national politicians regularly denounce for threatening their constituents' survival, is one for which the unelected and virtually unaccountable Commission is especially well suited. Member state capitals are glad to leave the dirty work to Brussels.[8]

Fighting entrenched national interests in the name of competition is something any fan of the free market will cheer. But when it comes to mergers and allegedly monopolistic practices, the Commission's main goal seems not to be safeguarding market processes, but protecting smaller companies from industry leaders. Whereas American antitrust authorities will normally approve a merger that leaves one firm dominating the market, so long as the merger promises to create efficiencies that will benefit customers, the Commission assumes that any such benefits will vanish as soon as the dominant company can crush its rivals. It was on these grounds that the Commission ruled out the GE-Honeywell merger, even while it acknowledged that the deal would have led to lower prices. In other words, society

cannot trust the market alone to sort out the worthiest competitors—
that requires the supervision of expert bureaucrats in Brussels. This
assumption lies behind more recent Commission decisions that car
manufacturers may not form exclusive relationships with independent dealers, or that Coca-Cola beverage coolers must also include
Pepsi products.

One commentator has summed up the dirigiste (or "Colbertist")
world-view in the maxim, "everything not authorized is prohibited."[9]
This could also be a concise statement of the "precautionary principle," an official precept of EU law with special relevance for environmental and consumer protection regulation. The precautionary
principle in effect presumes a product or substance dangerous unless
proven safe. The burden of proof lies on businesses seeking to sell or
use the materials in question, giving enforcement authorities discre-
tion to ban substances without evidence of risk.

The precautionary principle lies at the heart of the
Commission's proposed chemicals regime, known as REACH
(Registration, Evaluation, and Authorization of Chemicals), which
would require the registration and testing of 30,000 substances, even
those which there is no reason to believe are toxic. REACH would
also require manufacturers to disclose proprietary information about
applications of chemicals: trade secrets that are often key to a firm's
competitiveness. The precautionary principle is likewise the ratio-
nale for restrictions on the sale of hormone-treated beef and biotech
food products.

Ironically enough, such regulatory zeal draws strength from
Europeans' mistrust of their regulatory authorities. After mishandled
crises over bovine spongiform encephalopathy (BSE, or "mad cow
disease"), tainted blood, and dioxin-contaminated animal feed, to
name just three, Europeans are understandably prone to err on the
side of precaution. But by promoting the illusion that risk can be
eliminated—rather than balanced against other risks and costs, in a
world where danger is inevitable—application of the precautionary
principle can lead to unintended consequences. For example, under
an EU directive requiring animals to be inspected by a veterinarian
before slaughter, even absent signs of illness, economies of scale dic-
tate transporting the animals to large regional processing plants,

rather than hire a vet for every small local abattoir. Aside from the suffering that transportation causes the animals (a problem that other EU rules exist to correct), this practice has led to the quicker and wider spread of hoof-and-mouth disease.[10]

Such regulation also presents obvious opportunities for protectionism. Critics have suggested that European resistance to biotech foods springs not only from worries about the environment but also from a desire to shield Europe's less advanced farmers from high-tech American competition.

American regulation can cause problems for European companies, of course. Several EU firms have stopped listing their securities on the U.S. stock market to avoid the costly and time-consuming auditing procedures required by the Sarbanes-Oxley Act. Many in Europe see "Sarbox" as America's overreaction to the Enron scandal, and argue that existing European rules on corporate governance are adequate to safeguard the interests of shareholders. (The British financial industry is able to look on the bright side, since the Act has enhanced the attraction of the London Stock Exchange to non-European firms, in China and elsewhere, which might otherwise have listed in New York.)

In general, however, Washington regulates far less than Brussels or the EU member states; and when it does regulate, it is less likely to act on the principle of precaution. Instead of making rules to provide for every contingency imaginable, we Americans prefer to thrash things out in court. The British philosopher Roger Scruton argues that, "American litigiousness has the same effect as the European nanny state," by boosting the cost and complexity of activities ranging from major surgery to a child's visit to the playground.[11] This could become a European concern as well, as the global nature of business makes foreigners increasingly subject to the authority of U.S. courts, where damage awards are much higher than in Europe and where lawyers will work for a percentage of the prospective winnings (a practice banned in much of the EU). Yet litigation is not comparable to regulation as an instrument of economic nationalism, precisely because it does not favor local parties. In 2004, for instance, a group of U.S. tort lawyers brought a class-action suit against German, Austrian, and American companies for a cable-car accident that had occurred in the Austrian Alps. The vast majority of the plaintiffs were not Americans.

Within the EU, regulations long protected national industries from foreign competition. Governments first lifted tariffs and quotas only to replace them with national product standards, which they used to keep out other countries' merchandise. For instance, Germany banned a French liqueur called Cassis de Dijon on the grounds that its alcohol content was too low. Italy required that car windshields be laminated, whereas Germany specified tempered glass, one of many such technical differences that impeded development of a single market in automobiles.[12]

To prevent this practice, international committees today set detailed industrial standards for the entire EU, while the Commission sets the so-called "minimum standards." These standards can seem not so very minimal, however. A notorious seven-page Commission regulation on banana quality stipulates that the fruit must be at least fourteen centimeters in length, "along the convex face, from the blossom end to the point where the peduncle joins the crown," and at least twenty-seven millimeters thick "between the lateral faces and the middle, [measured] perpendicularly to the longitudinal axis."[13]

The dirigistes in the EU seek to "harmonize" (in Brussels parlance) far more than product standards; they would impose common policies in many areas, including taxation and welfare. But Britain has always insisted on national vetoes in both these matters and has thus preserved the possibility of tax and policy competition among the member states. That freedom became especially relevant after the accession in 2004 of the low-tax, pro-business states of Central and Eastern Europe.

Though critics condemn such diversity as "social dumping" and a "race to the bottom," the single market's dynamism depends on it. As the economist Martin Wolf explains:

> All monopoly is dangerous. This is just as true of most governmental monopolies, as it is of private ones. Competition among regulatory regimes restrains the excesses of each. The danger in the EU is that the countries that have conceded high levels of regulation or taxation at home wish to shackle their rivals. When they have succeeded, they will concede still higher levels of regulation. There will then be a steady ratcheting up of market-distorting regulations.[14]

The only effective brake on such a tendency is competition among the member states. But the application of market logic to the realm of government policy is anathema to the dirigiste value system.

Harnessing Globalization—and America

Competition in tax and regulation means that a dirigiste regime cannot trade freely with more liberal regimes without compromising on its interventionist program at home. The pressure of competition will force the regime to liberalize, to keep its businesses from failing or fleeing.

Of course, the dirigiste regime can try hiding behind tariffs and other trade barriers. But that means higher prices and fewer choices for companies and consumers at home. Moreover, in a globalized economy dominated by multinational companies, simple protectionism is increasingly unworkable, since it's often impossible to distinguish local industry from the foreign competition.

A more promising strategy for such a regime is to get other nations to adopt its policies. That is the logic behind harmonization within the EU's single market. And it is why the EU promotes its way of regulation to the rest of the world. The only way to make sure that EU standards do not put European industry at a competitive disadvantage is to ensure that industry around the world has to work to those same standards.

One of the "overarching objectives" of the EU's environmental policy, according to an official Commission document, is "to promote Community environmental standards and approaches at international and global levels."[15] The EU uses practical incentives as well as persuasion to spread its regulations and standards. Whereas companies all over the world must pay a fee to the American authorities before they may adopt U.S. industrial standards for their products, the EU subsidizes the sale of European standards in many developing nations, making these standards free to companies there. And of course there is the leverage of market access, which has driven so many farmers outside of Europe to eschew planting biotech crops even for domestic consumption.

All this matters to the U.S. because it means that American exporters of dishwashers, electric razors, or any other products must now conform to EU regulations, not only in Europe, but increasingly in other markets too. That's why American-made aftershave lotion has not contained ethanol since the EU banned it, and why GE-brand X-ray machines now meet dosage standards set by Brussels.[16] At least thirteen countries outside the EU now use European industrial standards extensively or exclusively; and the EU is working hard to sign up China and India, and eventually the rest of the world.

For the dirigiste party within the EU, this is an essential part of the plan. According to Pascal Lamy, the French Socialist who served as the EU's top trade negotiator until 2004 and is now director-general of the World Trade Organization, the world suffers from "a deficit of global rules." Since pollution, poverty, and disease do not respect national borders in a globalized economy, the answer is "global governance," in the multilateral form of which the EU itself is the most advanced example. "The main role of the European Union in international affairs, both political and economical, must be to give teeth and to give bite to this multilateralism," Lamy has said, quoting the words of Jean Monnet that the EU is "nothing but a step towards the organization of tomorrow's world."

Lamy is not terribly specific about the policies of his envisioned global governance, but they do not sound liberal to me. His metaphors evoke forceful intervention: he wants to "harness," "manage," and "steer globalization"; he speaks of capitalism as a "torrent" and a "directionless stream" that must be channeled and dammed up. The former Commissioner's inclinations are even clearer in his comments on the EU itself. He calls for a "real harmonization of our economic and budgetary policies," and an end to tax competition. Since the EU is Lamy's "laboratory and model" for global governance, this suggests what he has in mind for the rest of the world.[17]

Though Lamy does not say so, the hardest part of realizing his vision will be getting the U.S. to go along. As the other great world economy, and still a more dynamic one than Europe, America is an indispensable participant in any scheme of global governance. As a relatively liberal regime, the U.S. is the foremost obstacle to the imposition of global dirigisme. "Harnessing globalization" therefore means harnessing America.

Using the leverage of its huge market, the EU is already beginning to impose its norms of environmental regulation and antitrust law on the world's richest and most powerful nation. But its most effective instrument for checking America's economic power could turn out to be the common currency.

"The historical significance of the euro is to construct a bipolar economy in the world," said European Commission President Romano Prodi, upon the currency's launch on January 1, 2002. "There are two poles now: the dollar, and the euro." Or as Robert Mundell, the Nobel-prize-winning Canadian economist known as "father of the euro" (who first argued for a common European currency in 1969), has explained to me, the "political" motivation behind the euro was the desire to establish a "balance of powers" in the international monetary system.

As an alternative global reserve currency, the euro lets European nations share in advantages that for most of the twentieth century were enjoyed exclusively by the United States. One of these advantages has been the U.S. government's ability to finance huge budget deficits with foreign money. All those dollar reserves sitting in Chinese and Japanese banks have been like checks from the U.S. Treasury that no one expected would ever be cashed; the money was reinvested in U.S. Treasury bonds, allowing our government to borrow it at below-market rates. Now some of those checks are being cashed, as foreigners balance their dollar reserves with euros; and Eurobonds are competing with Treasury securities, forcing the U.S. to pay higher rates of interest.

The euro also aggravates the general problem of Americans' indebtedness, otherwise known as the "current account deficit." Professor Mundell explains: "The U.S. has gone from being the biggest creditor nation to being the biggest debtor nation by far. As that mounts, eventually there comes a point at which the dollar becomes suspect," and foreign lenders move more and more of their assets into gold or euros.

The potential for politically motivated manipulation of such a situation is obvious. "Something that Americans will have to realize is that one of the motives of the euro is anti-Americanism," warned

Norman Lamont, a former British chancellor of the exchequer, in 1999. We might recall that French President Charles de Gaulle launched a public campaign to end the "hegemony of the dollar" in 1965, a major factor in events that forced President Richard Nixon to take the dollar off the gold standard six years later.

Yet Professor Mundell regards any sort of "monetary war" between Europe and America as "extremely unlikely, because the costs of it are so horrendous that any kind of hint about that could create enormous instability in the markets, and it would be very dangerous" for both sides. More conceivable is that third powers would act to strengthen the euro, in order to protest American foreign policy or simply to weaken the United States. Insurgents in Iraq have actually called on the world to "stop using the dollar, use the euro." Russian President Vladimir Putin and at least one OPEC official have raised the possibility of pricing their countries' oil production in euros instead of dollars. If any major oil producer such as Saudi Arabia were ever to do so, Professor Mundell says, that would provoke a significant devaluation of the dollar.

New Europe Rising?

Pascal Lamy's dirigiste vision of global governance is so clearly at odds with the American system, you might think it makes transatlantic conflict inevitable. Yet Europe right now is going through dramatic social, political, and economic changes that will affect the way the EU is run. These changes could bring Europe closer to American ways of doing and regulating business, and lead to greater harmony and cooperation between us.

The current European Commission under José Manuel Barroso, who began a five-year term in late 2004, is markedly more focused than its predecessors on economic competitiveness. At our first meeting shortly after he took office, President Barroso made clear to me his determination to make the EU an easier place to do business, an intention he also signaled by elevating the Commissioner for Enterprise to the status of Vice-President. Nor is it an accident that he put the Commission's key economic portfolios, for trade, competition, and the internal market, in the hands of people with strong ties to business, and hailing from member states with traditions of economic liberalism: Britain, Holland, and Ireland, respectively. Barroso, who as prime minister of Portugal from 2002 to 2004 oversaw liberalizing and tax-cutting reforms in his country, is determined to reduce Europe's regulatory burden on enterprise, not only by making EU rules simpler and easier to comply with—that is, by cutting the red tape—but by producing less regulation in the first place.

President Barroso and his colleagues know that Europe must grow more productive in order to avoid a looming demographic crisis. Europeans are having fewer children and therefore their population is growing older. The EU fertility rate in 2005 was 1.48 children per woman (compared to 2.08 in the U.S), where the "replacement" level which ensures a stable population is 2.1. This means that ever-fewer European workers will be paying for the pensions and health care of ever-more-numerous retirees. Moreover, Europe's growth has for years lagged behind America's. In 2004, the EU's GDP increased by only 1 percent (compared with 3 percent in the U.S.), a trend that cannot continue if Europe hopes to support its aged. This problem will require a number of solutions, including immigration and pension reform, but clearly one major element will be getting more people to work.

Yet Barroso and his Commission also know that there is little they can do to solve the problem of job creation, since labor market regulation and welfare policies are mostly determined by the member states, not Brussels. Fortunately, there has been progress in this area on the national level. In 2005, Germany reformed its program of state-funded unemployment benefits to increase incentives for the jobless to find and accept work. The same year, France began letting employees work longer than the thirty-five-hour week instituted by a Socialist government in 1998. While limiting work hours in theory boosts employment by requiring companies to hire more people for the same tasks, it raises the costs of doing business and thus inhibits the creation of new jobs (France's unemployment rate actually rose after full implementation of the thirty-five-hour week), as do the regulations in so many EU countries that make it prohibitively expensive to fire or lay anyone off.

The strongest impetus for reform right now comes from the newest EU member states in Central and Eastern Europe, which have brought new competitive pressures to bear on the European labor market. An office temporary worker in Poland might cost an employer €3.50 per hour, compared to €18 in Italy or €25 in the Netherlands. And the skill level of Eastern workers is extremely high, even by comparison with Western Europe or the United States. One of the few happy legacies of Communism is a strong emphasis on math and science instruction, indispensable for industries based on information and communications technology. Estonia, Latvia, Poland, and Slovenia have higher percentages (58, 63, 56, and 61 percent respectively) of their high school graduates moving straight to postsecondary education than either France or Germany (54 and 46 percent—compared to 62 percent in the U.S.).[18] In response to this competition, the senior fifteen EU member states have all imposed waiting periods, in some cases until 2011, before citizens of the newest members can travel freely to the west in search of work. This has naturally provoked resentment in the Central and Eastern countries, but at the same time, has given Western businesses an added incentive to relocate there.

Lower tax rates and more liberal labor policies in these countries are other obvious draws for Western business. As former prime minister of Estonia Mart Laar noted in 2003, the year before enlargement: "In the new member states, even the most left-wing governments are significantly more free-market oriented than the most right-wing governments among the current members."[19] Slovakia, with a flat tax of 19 percent on both individual and corporate income, has been dubbed "Monte Carlo on the Danube," while Estonia's corporate tax rate of zero—yes, zero—percent has won it the less glamorous title of "the Delaware of Europe." On the eve of enlargement, the median corporate tax rate in the ten new member states was 19 percent, compared to 33 percent in the older members and 38 percent in Germany, prompting one investment banker to observe: "What's to stop Nokia from incorporating in Estonia? Or BMW in Slovakia?"[20]

The pressure of competition was producing results even before it actually started. Austria got ready for enlargement by cutting its corporate tax rate from 34 percent to 25 percent, and Finland by cutting its tax on spirits (a more significant levy than it may sound) by 30 percent. Starting in the summer of 2004, German and French labor unions agreed to work longer hours for the same pay, after Siemens, Opel, Daimler, Bosch, and other manufacturers threatened to move production to the east. The unions knew that the employers were not bluffing. By the time of enlargement, France's Peugeot Citroën and Germany's Volkswagen had already built automobile factories in Slovakia, and Korea's Kia (an affiliate of Hyundai) had chosen Slovakia for its first plant outside of Asia.

Dirigiste regimes were not amused. France and Germany called for harmonization of corporate tax rates throughout the EU; and German Chancellor Gerhard Schröder threatened to punish "fiscal dumping" by cutting EU development aid to the new members. The French and German governments have both opposed the Commission's proposal to form a single market in services, including education, health care, and construction, claiming that this would open the door to "social dumping," with the longer-established member states forced to cut social services and loosen worker protections in order to compete against the post-Communist countries in a "race to the bottom."

Behind such complaints lies the assumption that, given a choice, businesses will automatically move to the country offering the lowest tax rates and cheapest labor. If true, this would mean that Western European nations must choose between trading freely with more liberal regimes, or maintaining a generous welfare state— between joining the world of American-style "raw capitalism," or preserving "social solidarity." Lamy has said that global governance is necessary to save the "European social model." In other words, countries offering their citizens universal health care, free university education, and hefty unemployment benefits cannot hope to compete in a global economy, or even in an integrated Europe, without leveling the playing field by ensuring that all their commercial partners adopt similar policies.

But this assumption ignores the contrary examples of the EU's own Scandinavian members. Sweden has long been the archetypal welfare state; and like it, Denmark and Finland continue to provide their citizens with "cradle-to-grave" social services, including medical care, lengthy paid maternity (or paternity) leave, and generous unemployment insurance. At the same time, these nations are among the EU's most enthusiastic free traders, evidently finding little threat to their systems from lower-cost foreign competition. Home to such world-class companies as Volvo, Eriksson, and Nokia, the Scandinavian countries have done very well indeed by globalization. One hears little talk from them about harmonizing EU tax rates or labor regulations. (These generalizations apply almost equally well to Norway, which though not an EU member, participates in the single market as part of the associated European Economic Area.)

How do the Scandinavians manage to reconcile the apparently opposed goals of global free trade and the European social model? Americans may be surprised to learn that despite all their welfare provisions, the economic regimes of these countries are in many respects highly liberal. All rank in the highest category of "free" in the 2005 edition of *The Index of Economic Freedom*, published annually by the Heritage Foundation and *The Wall Street Journal*. According to the index, Denmark actually has a freer economy than the U.S., with its government imposing less of a regulatory burden on business; and the Swedish government poses fewer obstacles to foreign investment than Washington does. Most surprising of all, perhaps, is that Finland, Denmark, and Sweden have lower corporate tax rates than the U.S., and that as of 2004, Danes pay lower rates of personal income taxes than Americans do.

All of these nations have to one degree or another instituted liberalizing reforms over the last decade, but this does not mean that they have abandoned the welfare state. Rather, they are trying to ensure its survival. They understand that costly social services depend on national businesses remaining internationally competitive. At the same time, they know that well-run public services can enhance economic competitiveness. An educated workforce is an incomparable commercial asset, and the products of Scandinavian public schools have scored well above the average—and far above American students—on the International Student Assessment (PISA).[21] Many companies, including the European affiliates of American firms, find it simpler and ultimately cheaper to pay taxes for national health insurance than to provide their employees with private medical coverage. Voters, too, are evidently willing to pay high taxes if they feel they are getting their money's worth. Despite the proximity of Estonia and other low tax regimes just across the Baltic Sea, Sweden still has one of the highest top rates of personal income tax in the developed world, 60 percent.

Whether such policies will survive if European nations start spending more on their military defense (see chapter 4) is a crucial question. But right now, the biggest challenge to survival of the European welfare state is immigration. As two Harvard economists have documented in a recent transatlantic study, people tend to favor state-enforced income redistribution when the beneficiaries are members of their same race, but not otherwise. The economists use this finding to explain why government spending is 50 percent higher in continental Europe than in the far more ethnically mixed United States. A British Member of Parliament, David Willetts, has made a similar point with regard to culture: "You can have a Swedish welfare state provided that you are a homogenous society with intensely shared values. In the U.S. you have a very diverse, individualistic society where people feel fewer obligations to fellow citizens."[22]

That's a bleak way to put it, but it's not surprising that a more diverse society would inspire a more limited sense of what Europeans call "social solidarity." Opponents of immigration in Europe frequently complain—despite all the evidence of hardworking foreigners in their midst—of an alien "invasion" seeking to live off the public dole. As the EU becomes more ethnically mixed, it will be no surprise if member states scale back welfare spending and therefore government in general. (This doesn't necessarily mean Europeans will become less generous. The same Harvard study shows that Americans give twelve times as much to charity per capita as Europeans do.)

There is no one formula for national success in the global economy. Both a welfare state such as Sweden and a low-tax, laissez-faire regime such as Hong Kong can thrive. Globalization can accommodate different sets of social choices. The vital thing is that government allow as much freedom as possible for entrepreneurial initiative and growth. The test of an economy's freedom is its success in free international trade, whereas a dirigiste regime naturally seeks, ultimately in vain, to control and shield itself from the market forces on which prosperity depends. France and Germany, whose rates of GDP growth trail those of more liberal EU member states, must travel much farther along the path of economic reform. But that need not mean becoming copies of the United States. It could mean becoming more like Denmark, Finland, or Sweden.

The pressure for reform within EU member states has accelerated with the arrival of the post-Communist countries; and the same is true on the supranational level, of economic policy made in Brussels. Enlargement has increased the number of farmers in the EU from 7 million to 11 million, but the fund for agricultural subsides has stayed the same, and is likely to get smaller. The fight over an ever-diminishing pie should lead to a scaling back of the Common Agricultural Policy, to the benefit of farmers in developing nations as well as the United States. "Structural funding," or development assistance to the poorer member states, is the second biggest item in the EU budget; but as the EU grows bigger, there is also less of this money to go around, making it more urgent for new and prospective members to adapt to the competitive pressures of the single market.

No less galvanizing than the new member states' pro-business policies is their pro-business *culture*, embodied in their young entrepreneurs. That's no coincidence. Many of the government officials doing most to facilitate growth in the new member states are friends and classmates of the most ambitious businessmen. Old enough to remember Communism but young enough to have grown up out of its shadow, this rising generation is unabashed in its embrace of the economic freedom that its parents and grandparents missed, and eager to make the most of the opportunities that the EU offers.

The rest of Europe should hope that their enthusiasm is catching. Only 4 percent of EU citizens started a company in the three years prior to enlargement, compared with 11 percent of Americans. That's a dismaying statistic for anyone who would like to see Europe innovate and grow. A Commission report in 2004 attributed the low number largely to a dearth of "entrepreneurial values."

Certainly, from the American perspective, Europeans don't care enough about creating wealth. No doubt the roots of this prejudice run deep. Europe's aristocratic past was not one that celebrated the self-made man; and neither was the more egalitarian Europe of the postwar era, which tended to denigrate ambition for personal riches. The contrast between Old World and New World attitudes to business was one big reason that I stayed in California as a young man rather than move back to Holland.

Yet government can do much to inhibit or encourage entrepreneurial initiative. Europe's unforgiving bankruptcy laws discourage risk-taking, which does nothing to attract the venture capital that start-ups need, nor to change a culture that treats failure as disgrace. In the U.S., an entrepreneur with an honest bankruptcy on his record can get a second (or a third, or a fourth) chance. In France or Germany, bankruptcy is simply the end. More generally, given all the taxes, rules, and red tape that many European business people must still contend with, it's much harder to make money honestly than in the U.S.; so it's no wonder that many Europeans view commercial success with suspicion. Changing those attitudes will require an EU that fosters rather than suppresses competition.

Another deep-rooted difference between Europeans and Americans is the relative importance we place on leisure. When the future First Lady Abigail Adams visited Paris in the late eighteenth century, she remarked: "It is a matter of great speculation to me when these people labor." More than a century later, Thomas Edison, the archetypal American entrepreneur as well as a great inventor, visited the French capital and was scandalized by "the absolute laziness of everybody over here. When do these people work? What do they work at? People here seem to have established an elaborate system of loafing. I don't understand it at all."[23] Today Europeans take much more paid vacation (as many as forty-two days a year in Italy, compared to sixteen in the U.S.) and put in shorter weeks than Americans; so that in 2003, employees in the Netherlands worked an average of 438 hours less than their counterparts in the States.[24]

Yet it seems to me that attitudes are shifting on both sides of the Atlantic. The business students and young managers and entrepreneurs I have met all over Europe, whether they come from Italy or Poland, are impatient with the rigid hierarchies of the past and eager to succeed in a global business environment, which they know takes lots of work. At the same time, I see Americans of my children's thirtysomething generation and younger placing more emphasis on quality of life, including the time that they can spend with family. U.S. employers are responding to the needs of women employees in particular by making work schedules more flexible. And as a consequence of recent acquisitions of U.S. firms by European investors, increasing numbers of Americans are being exposed to European standards of working conditions and employment benefits. The coming years may see a surprising amount of convergence in the work practices of Americans and Europeans.[25]

Whatever the trends, the most productive societies as well as the happiest will be those that leave individuals as free as possible to make the trade-offs they need or desire between income and leisure. According to the World Database of Happiness, compiled by a Dutch scholar at the University of Rotterdam, nine European countries, seven of them EU member states, outrank the U.S. in terms of "how much people enjoy their life as a whole." Significantly, all but one of these countries also rank in the highest category of *The Index of Economic Freedom*. (The exception is Malta, but after all, it would be hard *not* to be happy on such a beautiful Mediterranean island.)[26]

The Choice

During the Convention on the Future of Europe, the assembly that met for sixteen months in 2002 and 2003 to put together a constitution for the EU, delegations from France and Germany proposed making EU taxation policy subject to majority voting by the member states. Doing so would have taken taxation out of the hands of national governments, putting an end to tax competition. Britain, true to its liberal traditions, opposed the measure, as did the ten incoming members. That much surprised no one. What was startling was the breadth of opposition: the measure was defeated 20–6.[27]

This showed that Britain and the post-Communist countries were not part of a recalcitrant minority but in the vanguard of a rising movement, a movement to make the EU more economically liberal, and to reassert the authority of national governments as the ultimate arbiters of law and policy. These two goals are inextricably related, since a dirigiste EU is necessarily one dominated by supranational authorities. It's no coincidence that the Commission's pro-business President Barroso has insisted, to much consternation in Brussels, that the "basic legitimacy of our union is the member states," and has characterized those who would remove national vetoes on foreign and economic policy as "naive federalists."

Failure to ratify the proposed constitution could actually improve the odds for liberalizing the EU by halting the tendency toward more supranational economic regulation and thus preserving the possibility of tax and policy competition—which is the only effective way to promote the market-based reforms that Europe needs in order to grow.

Many are eager to take up the battle. Even before the accession of the Central and Eastern states, Britain was not alone in defending the free market. Ireland has boomed in the last decade and a half, thanks largely to tax cuts and limited government spending. Spain, Denmark, and the Netherlands have loosened regulation in many areas and seen their economies grow more dynamic as a result. Even Germany has made it tougher to qualify for jobless benefits as an incentive to work. Now, owing largely to competition from the new member states, *all* EU countries have lower corporate tax rates than the U.S.—a situation which the *Wall Street Journal* has predicted is "likely to prompt U.S. companies to expand there rather than at home." This raises the remarkable possibility that America might soon find itself following Europe's liberalizing lead.

Most encouragingly, the leaders of dirigiste France and Germany have recognized the need to counter Brussels's interventionism. In an unprecedented move, they joined in September 2003 with British Prime Minister Tony Blair in criticizing the proposed REACH chemicals regime as "too bureaucratic and unnecessarily complicated," and urging the Commission to make it more business friendly. (In early 2005, Günter Verheugen, Vice President of the Commission with the portfolio for enterprise, vowed to amend that legislation to reduce its burden on industry.)

Paris and Berlin nevertheless remain wed to dirigisme on their home turf. Despite opposition from Brussels, the French government continues to intervene in favor of troubled national champions, such as Alstom and computer maker Bull, and to fend off foreign takeovers of French firms, such as the pharmaceutical giant Aventis. Gerhard Schröder's government has angered the Commission by gutting legislation that would have made it easier for foreign investors to take over EU firms, and by maintaining a law that keeps Volkswagen under the control of the German state of Lower Saxony. As noted above, France and Germany are also the strongest opponents of the Commission's proposal to liberalize the EU's market in services.

Yet in their incorrigible attachment to dirigiste practices, as in their repeated flouting of deficit limits for the euro zone, Germany and France have ironically acted as forces for liberalism within the EU, by reaffirming the power of national governments to set economic policy.

No less ironic, the French Left's victorious campaign against the constitution as an "ultraliberal" document could well turn out to have served the cause of liberalism, by checking the power of the dirigistes in Brussels.

All these events have made it possible to imagine the EU as a "politically and economically ever more diverse club":

> Countries pursuing the right domestic tax, welfare, and labor market policies will be rewarded with (physical and human) capital inflows, stronger growth, and lower unemployment, and will serve as a role model for others. Eventually, a competitive process of dynamic benchmarking will lift the tide for all members willing and able to play the game and should result in a less regulated and stronger European economy.[28]

This would of course mean the demise of the dirigiste vision for the EU. Indeed, the French historian and economist Nicolas Baverez has already heralded the "triumph of the British conception of Europe [as] a free-trade zone regulated only by competition."[29]

Yet it is too soon for liberals to declare victory. Whatever the ideological complexion of the current slate of commissioners, dirigistes predominate overwhelmingly among the career civil servants who actually write the legislation that comes out of Brussels. They already have over 80,000 pages of EU law to back them up, and the European Court of Justice has ruled that EU regulations override national rules except when the latter are stricter. Dirigistes have inherited the prestige of the EU's founders, and they draw support from the large center-left opposition in the current European Parliament, members of which have branded the Barroso agenda "neoliberal" and even "neo-conservative." Perhaps most important, dirigisme is still the only language of European integration. Rhetoric, it has been observed, has powerful political consequences because it builds up expectations.[30] As long as liberals offer no stirring alternatives to calls for "social solidarity" and "global governance," their position remains merely negative or defensive. Here, too, the Central and Eastern nations, with their all-too-recent memories of hollow Communist slogans and disastrous central planning, and their still-fresh appreciation of economic freedom, will play an essential role.

The choice for a liberal or a dirigiste EU is one that Europeans will make for themselves. The U.S. has no direct part in the debate, yet we have an enormous stake in its outcome. Our business and political leaders must do all they can to encourage those who seek an EU where nations as well as businesses are free to compete.

Notes

1. During a dispute over U.S. tariffs on imported steel, the EU threatened sanctions targeted at products from American states deemed crucial to the reelection of President George W. Bush. The sanctions were never imposed, since the steel dispute was resolved in late 2003, but the Commission revived the threat the following spring during another trade clash.

2. Nye, Joseph S., Jr., *The Paradox of American Power*, Oxford: Oxford University Press, 2002, pp. 19, 20.

3. Quinlan, Joseph P., and Daniel S. Hamilton, *Partners in Prosperity: The Changing Geography of the Transatlantic Economy*, Washington, D.C.: Center for Transatlantic Relations, 2004, pp. xi–xvii.

4. Dedman, Martin J., *The Origins and Development of the European Union 1945–95*, London and New York: Routledge, 1996, pp. 26, 27, 99, 100.

5. Treaty Establishing the European Community, as Amended by Subsequent Treaties, Rome, March 25, 1957. Article 3.1(h) EC. http://europa.eu.int/eur-lex/lex/en/treaties/index.htm.

6. Dedman, pp. 97, 103.

7. De Jonquières, Guy, "Oxfam says EU sugar trade is hurting the poor," *Financial Times*, April 13, 2004.

8. *European* champions are of course another story. The multinational conglomerate Airbus has surpassed America's Boeing as the world's largest maker of commercial aircraft with significant help from the competition authority and other parts of the European Commission.

9. De Jasay, "Between Colbert and Adam Smith," *Cato Journal*, 21: 3 (Winter 2002), pp. 359–367.

10. Scruton, Roger, "The Cult of Precaution," *The National Interest*, 76 (Summer 2004), pp. 148–154, 150.

11. Scruton, pp. 152, 153.

12. Dedman, pp. 125, 126.

13. "Commission Regulation (EC) No 2257/94 of 16 September 1994 laying down quality standards for bananas," p. 5. http://europa.eu.int/smartapi/cgi/sga_doc?smartapi!celexapi!prod!CELEXnumdoc&lg=en&numdoc=31994R2257&model=guicheti.

14. Wolf, Martin, "No way to create a dynamic Europe," *Financial Times*, April 6, 2004.

15. Environment Directorate General, *2003 Management Plan*, p. 7.

16. Reid, T. R., *The United States of Europe: The New Superpower and the End of American Supremacy*, New York: Penguin, 2004, pp. 232, 235.

17. Lamy, Pascal, "Is the enlarged EU an economic superpower?" Oxford, March 10, 2004, http://europa.eu.int/comm/commissioners/lamy/speeches_articles/spla215_en.htm; "What Europe for this world?" Grandes Conférences Catholiques—Brussels, March 24, 2003, http://europa.eu.int/comm/commissioners/lamy/speeches_articles/spla163_en.htm; "Les politiques communes et l'Europe dans la mondialisation," Institut de France—Académie des Sciences morales et politiques, Paris, March 29, 2004, http://europa.eu.int/comm/commissioners/lamy/speeches_articles/spla218_fr.htm.

18. Bowers, David, *EU Enlargement*, Merrill Lynch, April 6, 2004, pp. 3, 16; National Center for Education Statistics (NCES), *The Condition of Education 2003*, NCES 2003–067, Washington, D.C.: U.S. Department of Education, 2003, appendix table 1-19.

19. Laar, Mart, "New Members Will Make the EU More Competitive," *European Affairs*, 4: 3 (Summer/Fall 2003), pp. 60–63, 60; and "New Europe Won't 'Keep Quiet' Until All Europe Is New," *The Wall Street Journal Europe*, February 19, 2003.

20. Taino, Danilo, "E la Slovacchia diventò la Montecarlo della Ue," *Corriere Della Sera*, April, p. 9; Bowers, pp. 4, 11.

21. "First Results from PISA 2003: Executive Summary," Paris: OECD, 2004, p. 9, http://www.pisa.oecd.org/dataoecd/1/63/34002454.pdf.

22. Alesina, Alberto, and Edward Glaeser, *Fighting Poverty in the U.S. and Europe: A World of Difference*, Oxford: Oxford University Press, 2004; Goodhart, David, "Too diverse?" *Prospect*, February 2004.

23. King, Florence, "Edison: Inventing the Century," *The American Spectator*, May 1995; Maslin, Janet, "Yep, When Good Americans Die, They Still Go to Paris," *The New York Times*, April 15, 2004, p. 7.

24. Stelzer, Irwin M., "European Holiday," *The Daily Standard*, September 15, 2003; *OECD Employment Outlook 2004*, Paris: OECD, 2004, p. 312.

25. Meiksins, Peter, and Peter Whalley, "Should Europe work more, or America less?" *International Herald Tribune*, August 11, 2004.

26. On a happiness scale of 0 to 10, the results were 8 for Denmark, Malta, and Switzerland (the three highest-scoring nations in the world); 7.8 for Iceland and Ireland; 7.6 for Luxembourg and the Netherlands; 7.5 for Finland and Sweden. The U.S. score was 7.4. Veenhoven, R., *Average happiness in 90 nations 1990–2000*, World Database of Happiness, RankReport 2004/1b, http://www2.eur.nl/fsw/research/happiness. In terms of economic freedom, Luxembourg, Ireland, Denmark, Iceland, and Switzerland all ranked above the U.S. within the highest category of "free." Miles, Marc, et al., *The Index of Economic Freedom*, Washington, D.C.: Heritage Books, 2005, Internet: http://www.heritage.org/research/features/index/countries.cfm.

27. The total number of votes exceeded twenty-five because, in addition to the fifteen current members and the ten accession states, several candidate states also participated in the Convention.

28. Fels, Joachim, "Breaking Up Euroland Might Not Be So Hard to Do," *The Wall Street Journal Europe*, February 5, 2004.

29. Bollaert, Baudoin, Marie-Laure Germon, and Alexis Lacroix, "Des Etats-Unis au tiers-monde," *Le Figaro*, February 9, 2004.

30. Alesina, Alberto, and Roberto Perotti, "The European Union: a politically incorrect view," November 2004, p. 7, http://post.economics.harvard.edu/faculty/alesina/papers/europeanunionfeb04.pdf.

FOUR

The European Union as a Geopolitical Superpower

W HILE THE GLOBAL reach of Europe's economic power is
beyond dispute, the European Union today is obviously not a
superpower in the usual sense, as a wielder of military might.

The EU does include two nations with nuclear arms, Britain and
France; but the twenty-five member states together spend less than
half as much on defense as does the United States, $186 billion ver-
sus $461 billion in the year 2004, and the difference is expected to
widen further over the second half of this decade.[1] This actually
understates the transatlantic "capability gap," since European nations
devote much more of their military budgets to personnel costs: over
70 percent in the cases of Belgium, Italy, and Portugal, compared
with 35 percent for the U.S. (While American service personnel
earn salaries comparable to those of their European counterparts, the
latter get more in health insurance, housing allowances, retirement
pay, and other benefits.) European nations thus have less money for
hardware acquisition: only 5.6 percent of the Portuguese defense budget goes to this purpose, compared with 25 percent of America's military spending.[2]

The EU member states actually have more men and women
under arms than the U.S.—1.9 million versus 1.6 million—but only
10 to 15 percent of the European forces are considered deployable,

whereas the U.S. can deploy three-quarters of its military personnel abroad. Linguistic differences, incompatible technology, and lack of cooperation among national commands have hampered the ability of European militaries to operate together, except within the structure of the U.S.-led NATO alliance. The debacle of Bosnia in 1992–1995, when Europeans proved unable to end the worst conflict on their own soil since World War II, inspired plans for an EU rapid reaction force of 60,000 troops, deployable on 60 days' notice for up to one year. Failure to meet that initiative's declared deadline of 2003 only further weakened Europe's military credibility. According to an oft-repeated quip, "Europe is an economic giant and a military dwarf."

Yet geopolitical power—the ability to influence the actions of other sovereign states—cannot be reduced to a capacity for making war. Throughout history, states have drawn geopolitical strength from their commerce, religion, ideology, language, and culture. In a world increasingly linked by economic globalization and information technology, the sources and forms of power in international relations are ever more varied.

The Harvard political scientist Joseph Nye has distinguished two broad categories of geopolitical power, soft and hard. These terms are frequently misunderstood to be nothing more than fancy names for carrots and sticks. But in Nye's scheme, both sticks and carrots—that is, military and economic might—are forms of hard or "command" power: the "ability to change what others *do*" through "coercion or inducement." Soft power, by contrast, is "co-optive power—the ability to shape what others *want* through the attractiveness of one's culture and values or the ability to manipulate the agenda of political choices" [emphases added].[3]

The EU today is a global power in both the hard and soft senses. Through the use of economic sanctions, financial assistance, and control of access to its vast single market, the EU's leaders can produce changes in the behavior of foreign regimes big and small. When they vote as a bloc in international organizations or come together to endorse international conventions, EU member states are unsurpassed in their ability to shape world opinion. The allure of joining the EU has induced aspiring member states to reform their own laws and public institutions. And the EU's historically unprecedented achievement of peacefully uniting long-hostile nations has made the organization a model and natural partner for regional groups around the globe.

Now the EU is developing a common foreign and security policy, to cultivate these strengths and enhance its military power. Success would make Europe a stronger partner for America in our common effort to make the world more stable and prosperous. Yet the path to this goal is a difficult one, and the next few years will be especially critical. America's leaders must recognize the EU's identity as a security organization, a new structure for brokering a European consensus on defense and security matters, with which the U.S. will increasingly have to deal. For their part, European leaders must not overemphasize the goal of military integration at the expense of their own security. Neither should they embrace an unrealistic faith in the power of mediation and diplomacy to avoid war; nor a doctrine of defense as the strictly reactive use of military force; nor a vision of the EU as a geopolitical counterweight to the power of the United States. Any of these courses would threaten to undermine the Atlantic alliance, to the grave detriment of America, Europe, and the world.

European Power, Hard and Soft

Europe's economic heft gives it leverage over the most powerful states. As I noted in the previous chapter, the EU has threatened to use trade sanctions to influence American presidential elections, though for commercial rather than political ends. Its embargo on arms sales to China, imposed after the Tiananmen massacre of 1989, was a factor in Beijing's gradually improving respect for human rights, until European leaders indicated the embargo's end might be imminent.

Sanctions are not, however, among the EU's favored instruments of foreign policy. Europeans have concluded that since governments can evade sanctions' effects, the real victims are likely to be innocent citizens of the targeted nations. True to the EU's origins as an effort at economic cooperation, its leaders prefer whenever possible to induce rather than coerce the behavior they want.

This preference explains the negotiating strategy adopted by Britain, France, and Germany in their joint effort, beginning in 2003, to halt Iran's development of nuclear weapons. In contrast to the American inclination to seek sanctions from the UN Security Council while reserving the option of military force, the Europeans have consistently sought to induce Tehran to shut down its uranium enrichment program by offering economic incentives, including possible support for Iranian membership in the World Trade Organization (WTO). Many Europeans complained that America's position undermined these negotiations.

My view, on the contrary, is that Iran would never have come to the table in the first place—any more than Libya's Colonel Gadhafi would have agreed, in talks with the British, to give up his weapons of mass destruction—without a "bad cop" America in Iraq. The European carrot would have been much less enticing without the American stick. But the U.S. has every interest in seeing the European efforts succeed. In March 2005, shortly after President Bush's visit to the EU institutions in Brussels, and as a direct result of his discussions there, the administration dropped objections to Iran's application to the WTO, in order to enhance Tehran's incentives to negotiate. As of this writing, the final results of talks were unknown.

In a less dramatic but far more extensive application of economic incentives, the EU has used grants of development assistance to nearby states in North Africa and the eastern Mediterranean—Algeria, Egypt, Israel, Jordan, Lebanon, Libya, Morocco, Syria, and Tunisia, as well as the Palestinian Authority—as a means of avoiding or meliorating conflicts over migration and disputed territory. It recently extended this policy to the former Soviet republics of Armenia, Azerbaijan, Belarus, Georgia, Moldova, and Ukraine. Northern EU member states have called for making this assistance conditional on recipients' respect for human rights, but southern members have resisted such a move, for fear of alienating the beneficiary governments.

The EU is the world's largest donor of "development assistance," intended to promote economic, social, and political development in poorer countries, and in 2003 it gave away (through the Commission and the separate member states) $44 billion—almost three times as much as the United States. The EU is also the top source of "humanitarian aid," such as emergency food, shelter, and medical care for the victims of natural or manmade crises, of which it provided 47 percent of the world total in 2001, compared with only 36 percent for the United States.[4] Such largesse buys good will and thus augments the EU's soft power even in regions where it has no obvious or direct geopolitical interest.

By subsidizing the free distribution of EU industrial standards to developing nations (see chapter 3), and by effectively requiring other countries, including the U.S., to adopt EU health, safety, and environmental regulations as a condition of access to its internal market, the EU expands its own potential export market. At the same time, it does something more subtle and consequential: it extends the reach of the EU's legal and political culture.

"By creating common standards that are implemented through national institutions, Europe can take over the world without becoming a magnet for hostility," proclaimed a poster at an officially sponsored EU exhibition in Brussels in late 2004, which also described the EU as the "world's first viral political space."[5] European integration as a virus? Even allowing for the irony and hyperbole of the Dutch art world (the show was designed by the firm of Rotterdam architect Rem Koolhaas and paid for by the government of the Netherlands), this is a fair description of one way in which the EU uses economic power to enhance its soft, agenda-setting power.

The EU can promulgate its standards and regulations without using economic incentives at all, by convincing other states that the European way is more appropriate to local conditions. For instance, several South American countries, including Argentina, Brazil, Chile, Peru, and Uruguay, have adopted the EU's legal framework on personal data privacy, largely on account of lobbying by Spain, a land with which most of them share language, cultural heritage, and—most crucially, with regard to privacy concerns—the recent experience of moving from dictatorship to democracy. Reflecting Europe's traumatic twentieth-century experiences with totalitarianism, the EU's Data Protection Directive strictly limits the ways in which the state may use personal information. As governments in an age of global terrorism struggle to balance security with the defense of civil liberties, the appeal of the EU's privacy framework—which Australia, Canada, and Japan have also adopted—significantly enhances European influence worldwide. Now this influence extends to the U.S. as well. After an extended dispute with the Commission over access to passenger data on transatlantic airline flights, the U.S. Department of Homeland Security finally agreed in 2004 to store such data for only three and a half years, instead of fifty as it had intended, and to use the data solely in connection with terrorism and other transnational crimes.

An "ability to manipulate the agenda of political choices" is a basic form of soft power, and nowhere is the EU more clearly able to do this than through international treaties, conventions, and organizations. America has felt the impact of this power more than once in the last several years.

The EU's unanimous support for the Kyoto Protocol on global warming turned that agreement into a virtual litmus test of environmental responsibility, muting debate over its scientific premises and discrediting alternative approaches to the balance between economic growth and protection of natural resources. As late as fall 2004 it seemed virtually impossible for economic reasons that Russia would sign on to Kyoto; and when it did so in February 2005, it was largely as a result of pressure from Europe.

Unlike the burgeoning industrial economies of Brazil, China, and India, which are exempt from the protocol, the U.S. has spent billions of dollars on the development of environmentally responsible technologies such as hydrogen-powered vehicles, electricity from renewable energy sources, and clean coal technology and on scientific research on climate change. Yet for refusing to ratify Kyoto, America has been cast in the role of reckless global polluter, at high though unquantifiable cost to our own soft power.

Since Europe is the birthplace of international jurisprudence, the EU's endorsement of the International Criminal Court (ICC) has made America seem an arrogant scofflaw for not signing on. Once that issue was framed as a choice between justice and impunity for war criminals, arguments that U.S. citizens deserve to be tried under the laws of our own Constitution went practically unheard. As a result, U.S. armed service members and civilians around the world are at risk of becoming targets of politicized prosecutions, without benefit of the checks and balances of the American judicial system.

Likewise, the EU's unqualified support for an international land-mine ban helped frame that issue as a simple choice between elimi-nating these ghastly weapons or continuing to use them recklessly. Although no nation has done more than the U.S. to rid the world of landmines, they remain an essential element in our defensive strat-egy in the demilitarized zone (DMZ) between North and South Korea. European unwillingness to compromise on this point has led to practical complications—local personnel at U.S. military bases in Japan may no longer handle the mines we store there—and has undermined the legitimacy of our Korean strategy.

When EU member states speak with one voice in international organizations, as they generally do at forums such as the Paris-based Organization for Economic Cooperation and Development (OECD), the Vienna-based Organization for Security and Co-operation in Europe (OSCE), and the Geneva-based United Nations Commission on Human Rights (UNCHR), they can set the terms of debate. Having one vote for every member state gives the EU an obvious edge in such contexts, as the U.S. learned in 2001, when the Europeans voted us off of the UNCHR for the first time since 1947. (Press reports at the time cast this event as a protest against American positions on the ICC, the landmine ban, and the death penalty. The real source of the dispute was simply the EU states' determination to have greater representation on the Commission.)

The EU's unparalleled record of integration gives it unique cred-ibility and prestige within international organizations, from the UN on down. Never mind that EU members ruthlessly defend their national interests within their own organization, flouting common policies (such as the cap on national budget deficits) when it suits them. As far as the rest of the world is concerned, Europeans are the premier guardians of the multilateral ideal.

The most magnificent example of European soft power is the EU itself. From the time of its founding, aspiring member states have made extensive changes in their systems in order to qualify. For the privilege of membership, the ten nations that joined in 2004 were willing to adopt an existing body of common EU law (the *acquis communautaire*) more than 80,000 pages long. Candidate countries Bulgaria and Romania are still making difficult economic and legal reforms to qualify. The most striking case is surely that of Turkey, which drastically revised laws and policies on such sensitive issues as the death penalty, the treatment of ethnic minorities, and the role of the military in politics, even before the EU had agreed to discuss the possibility of membership.

Although access to the EU's single market, agricultural subsidies, and structural funds are of course major incentives for countries to join, money alone cannot explain the EU's magnetic power. After all, Turkey has for years enjoyed a trade agreement with the EU that gives it most of the commercial advantages of membership. It could easily retain that status and spare itself the expense of conforming to the *acquis*, the humbling experience of supplicating Christian Europe for acceptance, and (assuming it is eventually accepted) the ultimate limits on its sovereignty. Indeed, several of the Turkish economists and political scientists whom I met on my visit to the country in 2004, though glad about the reforms undertaken to qualify for membership, thought that Turkey would be better off not joining the EU. Yet the Turkish government and (according to opinion surveys) 75 percent of the population see a value in belonging to Europe that makes it worth all the trouble.

Recent events in Ukraine demonstrate even more dramatically the EU's power of attraction—a power that has proved even greater than what some in the Union felt they could handle. Brussels had given the former Soviet republic no reason to hope that it could ever join the club. Romano Prodi, president of the European Commission until 2004, once said that Ukraine had "as much reason to be in the EU as New Zealand." In consigning Ukraine to its European Neighborhood Policy, the EU lumped it together with such obviously ineligible states as Syria and Tunisia. For his part, Russian President Vladimir Putin made it clear that Ukraine was to remain within the former superpower's sphere of economic and political influence.

Yet in late 2004, hundreds of thousands of ordinary Ukrainian citizens, inspired largely by a desire to join Europe, peacefully filled the streets of Kiev to prevent the stealing of a presidential election by the pro-Russian candidate. At negotiations between the besieged pro-Russian regime and the pro-western opposition, it was Alexander Kwasniewski and Valdas Adamkus, the presidents of EU member states Poland and Lithuania, and Javier Solana, the EU's High Representative for the Common Foreign and Security Policy, who acted as the primary mediators. In his ultimately successful campaign, the opposition leader Viktor Yushchenko proclaimed that joining the EU would be the top priority of his presidency, a goal he reaffirmed upon his inauguration in January 2005.

Whatever the economic and political challenges that Ukraine's European aspirations pose for the current member states, and regardless of whether or not Ukraine ultimately becomes a member, the EU's role as inspiration and guide for the "Orange Revolution" will stand as a stunning show of soft power.

The EU's magnetic pull extends far beyond the circle of potential members, to other continents where nations are engaged in their own efforts at economic or political integration. The Association of Southeast Asian Nations (ASEAN), founded in 1967 as a political and security organization and later the basis for a free trade area, agreed in 2003 to establish a European-style common market in goods, services, capital, and labor by 2020. Other organizations such as the African Union and the South American Community of Nations also look to Brussels for inspiration and guidance. Formal links with these younger organizations, and affinities with their institutional cultures, are potentially important avenues for European influence in these regions.

A Common Foreign and Security Policy

With all these sources of geopolitical power, does the EU need the traditional diplomatic and military apparatus of a nation-state? European leaders evidently think so, because for more than a decade they have been developing a common foreign policy, including provisions for the common defense.

The constitutional treaty signed in 2004 provides for a single foreign minister to speak on behalf of the entire Union, and a European External Action Service (EEAS) of diplomats to carry out that policy in foreign capitals around the world—both innovations that could still be instituted even though the constitution goes unratified. Italy's Foreign Minister and Vice Premier Gianfranco Fini has told me that he believes that, by the middle of the next decade, the EU will have its own seat on the UN Security Council and a single embassy representing all the EU member states in Washington. My guess is that it will take longer than that for France and Britain to give up their Security Council seats in favor of an EU representative, especially since Germany is now pushing for a seat of its own; but as the EU develops a more unified foreign policy, it will grow harder to justify giving Europe multiple votes at the UN and other international forums. Likewise, though European nations today are in no rush to close down their Washington embassies, EU delegations to other countries might soon start representing some of the smaller member states (such as Luxembourg, which has fewer than two dozen embassies of its own worldwide), establishing a trend that could eventually lead to a consolidated EU diplomatic service and therefore a more unified foreign policy.

The EU has already begun to assert a military identity, with its forces taking over peacekeeping duties from NATO troops in Macedonia (2003) and Bosnia (2004) and from UN troops in the Democratic Republic of Congo (2003), the first EU military operation outside Europe. In 2005, the first EU battle groups became operational: each is composed of 1,500 troops, capable of peacekeeping in hot spots up to 3,700 miles away on five to ten days' notice. Thirteen such battle groups, some of them multinational in composition, will be fully operational by 2007. Deployable two at a time, their purpose will be to enforce UN resolutions by providing stability for up to 120 days prior to the arrival of longer-term UN peacekeeping forces.

In 2004, the EU established the European Defense Agency to coordinate member states' procurement and equipment policies. Since one of Europe's major military weaknesses is in the area of "lift," the European conglomerate Airbus is building the A400M military transporter aircraft, each of which will be able to carry up to 120 fully equipped troops. The plane's speed and flexibility will make it suitable for battle group deployments as well as humanitarian relief missions.

The wider significance of these developments, all of which I witnessed during my tenure in Brussels, is that European nations are increasingly determined to take responsibility for their own security, which they know they can do only by acting in concert. The constitutional treaty signed in 2004 includes a "solidarity clause" committing all members to assist each other in the event of a terrorist attack. While the end of the Cold War in theory freed Europe from the need for American leadership, the Balkan wars of the 1990s revealed that Europeans still depended on the U.S. to keep the peace on their own soil. In response to those events, and as a natural outgrowth of its economic integration, the EU is now emerging as a geopolitical actor able and willing to act on its own. In the words of a 2004 report by a CIA think tank: "The EU, rather than NATO, will increasingly become the primary institution for Europe, and the role which Europeans shape for themselves on the world stage is most likely to be projected through it."[6]

The integration of the EU's foreign and defense policies is potentially good news for America. Despite our occasional differences of interpretation and approach, Europe and the U.S. have the same fundamental interests around the world. Among the top items on our common "to do" list are an end to Islamist terrorism, a halt to the proliferation of weapons of mass destruction, resolution of the Israeli-Palestinian conflict, reduction of global poverty and disease, prevention of failed states, and the expansion of economic and political freedom.

When the Europeans work with us, as they have done for example in Bosnia, Haiti, and Sudan, they contribute not only manpower and money, but also political support in the UN Security Council and other international arenas. China, Russia, and other powers are far less likely to oppose a position held by the U.S. when we have twenty-five European nation-states behind us. To the extent that integration makes the EU a more effective global actor, it can make our collaboration more successful on all fronts. As President Bush said in Brussels in 2005, "America supports a strong Europe, because we need a strong partner in the hard work of advancing freedom and peace in the world."

A common security and defense policy could spur European nations to spend more on their military, something which the U.S.

has long asked of our NATO allies (nineteen of which are also member of the EU). Voters in most European countries have shown scarce enthusiasm for increased spending on national defense, probably a reflection of their continent's disastrous twentieth-century experience with militarism and of fears that more money for arms would come at the expense of social services. But politicians should find it easier to win support for defense as a pan-European project to enhance continental security and promote international peace.

Europe's expanded military capabilities, if properly coordinated with existing NATO structures, would benefit the Atlantic alliance. A fully operational EU military force would reduce the likelihood of U.S. involvement in future conflicts that, like the Balkan wars, Europe considers within its sphere of influence. This would leave NATO free to undertake "out of area" operations, such as enforcing an eventual two-state solution to the Israeli-Palestinian conflict. Armed forces under an EU flag could also serve elsewhere alongside U.S troops.

America benefits more generally from European integration in the sense that a more united Europe is a more stable Europe. The addition of a foreign policy and security dimension to the EU should make internecine conflict even less likely than it is today. As the twentieth century tragically demonstrated, a divided Europe is a problem from which America cannot long remain aloof.

Yet the EU's assertion of a geopolitical identity is not a guaranteed boon to America. Because European integration has until recently focused inward—on the interests of European countries and the relationships among them—a foreign and security policy growing out of such preoccupations could tend to neglect transatlantic ties or even prove hostile to them. This would undermine America's security and ultimately Europe's own.

One danger to the Atlantic alliance lies in the very dynamic of European integration. Security and defense are matters of the highest possible stakes, and thus too sensitive to be exposed to "spill-over" from other policy areas (a process which I explained in chapter 1). Unless Europe's leaders carefully assess the impact that any common policy or initiative could have on the functioning of the transatlantic alliance, they risk letting integration proceed at the expense of security.

I saw an example of how integration by spill-over might damage the alliance during our negotiations over the Galileo satellite navigation system. This $4-billion-plus EU project is officially intended not for military purposes, but to produce a European competitor to the commercial version of the Pentagon's Global Positioning System (GPS). However, the band area in which EU planners originally chose to broadcast their signal was the same band area which the U.S. Defense Department had earmarked for an improved version of GPS, to be used in military communications and targeting technologies. The EU eventually agreed to move to another band area, which will permit a signal almost equally robust. But the compromise did not end debate over our efforts to preserve the technological edge in this critical area. The U.S. remains concerned that Galileo's commercial-grade service—which will be potentially available to our enemies—could undercut our ability to control the battlefield in future conflicts. China, which is contributing hundreds of millions of dollars to the project and participates in its planning, could also use the technology to improve the accuracy of its missiles. Other partners in Galileo include Israel, India, and Russia.

Another danger to the alliance lies in a European tendency to make integration, rather than security, the priority in the formation of common defense structures. This was the error made by leaders of France, Germany, Belgium, and Luxembourg in April of 2003, when they proposed establishing a joint military headquarters in the Brussels suburb of Tervuren. The EU already had an autonomous military planning cell at NATO headquarters in nearby Mons. Not a single EU military chief of staff favored a new headquarters, which would have siphoned off scarce planning personnel from national and NATO staffs at a time when European forces were busy in Afghanistan, the Balkans, and Iraq. Setting up an alternative EU headquarters would have contradicted the Berlin Plus Agreements, according to which the EU draws on NATO planning, support, and assets for any significant security mission. But coming as it did just a few weeks after the invasion of Iraq, and from the two EU nations— France and Germany—most opposed to the U.S.-led war against Saddam Hussein, it was clear that the Tervuren proposal (since withdrawn, and as of this writing not yet revived) was meant not as a practical military measure but a political gesture, an assertion of independence from American leadership.

Euro-Gaullist versus Euroatlanticist

Shortly after the Tervuren proposal was announced, the European Commissioner for Regional Affairs, Michel Barnier, later France's foreign minister, visited me at our embassy, acting as an unofficial emissary from Paris. Over lunch, Barnier reaffirmed France's ties of friendship with the U.S. and explained that one reason for building up the EU's military capabilities would actually be to earn America's confidence. But he also spoke of the need to "rebalance" the transatlantic relationship.

The word "rebalance" was unsettling in that it echoed the well-known French argument that a united Europe should act as a "counterweight" to American power. That idea has been an element, and at times a major strain, in France's foreign policy since the presidency of Charles de Gaulle (1958–1969).

While de Gaulle never doubted that the major threat to Western Europe during the Cold War came from the Soviet bloc, he also feared that France would be overwhelmed—politically, militarily, and culturally—by America. Therefore he pursued a strategy of alliance with Germany and of distance from America's close ally Britain, with the aim of making Europe under French leadership a center of power independent of the United States. In his own words: "What is the purpose of Europe? It should be to allow us to escape the domination of the Americans and the Russians. . . . Europe is a means for France to regain the stature she has lacked since Waterloo, as the first among the world's nations."[7]

One reason that de Gaulle repeatedly blackballed British participation in European integration was that he saw London as a potential Trojan horse for Washington. In defiance of U.S. policy of the day, de Gaulle gave diplomatic recognition to Communist China. Despite his own country's inglorious colonial record in Indochina, he loudly condemned the U.S. for its intervention in Vietnam. He launched a campaign to dethrone the American dollar as the world's unofficial reserve currency. And though France remained formally part of the Atlantic alliance, de Gaulle withdrew French forces from NATO's command structure, expelled NATO headquarters from France, and ordered American troops off his country's soil. (U.S. Secretary of Defense Dean Rusk responded by asking if the order also applied to American soldiers buried in French war cemeteries.)

Yet De Gaulle's anti-Americanism failed to acquire a following in Europe, most crucially in Germany. Immediately after ratifying a Franco-German friendship treaty in 1963, the West German parliament pointedly reaffirmed its commitment to the Atlantic alliance. For the rest of the Cold War, West Germany pursued a foreign policy of close alliance with France in internal European affairs and with America on wider geopolitical matters. Following de Gaulle's resignation in 1969, not even French governments took the counterweight strategy seriously. In the early 1980s, the Socialist President François Mitterrand proved an unlikely supporter of President Ronald Reagan's strategy against the Soviet Union, by urging the West German government to let the U.S. deploy Pershing and cruise missiles on German soil, despite strong domestic opposition.

Only after the fall of the Berlin Wall, with the U.S. security umbrella apparently no longer necessary, could Europeans seriously consider the desirability of counterbalancing American power. Since then, the French have reemerged as the principal exponents of what the British scholar-journalist Timothy Garton Ash has dubbed "Euro-Gaullism."[8]

Euro-Gaullist rhetoric heated up after the humiliation in Bosnia, where UN troops under a series of French commanders failed to stop Serb attacks on Muslims and Croats in a civil war which ultimately killed more than 270,000. A peace treaty was finally negotiated at a U.S. Air Force base in Dayton, Ohio, in late 1995, and the peace was kept by an American-led NATO mission. The year after Dayton, French President Chirac told an interviewer that Europe needed a "means to struggle against American hegemony." In 1999, after the U.S. led a successful war against Serb aggression in Kosovo, France's foreign minister declared: "We cannot accept either a politically unipolar world, nor a culturally uniform world, nor the unilateralism of a single hyperpower."

French talk of counterweights has lately given way to the more subtle metaphor of multipolarity. "The evolution of the world towards a multipolar situation is inevitable," said President Chirac in 2004. "There will be a great American pole, a great European pole, a Chinese one, an Indian one, eventually a South American pole." Though Chirac stipulated that it was essential that the "two poles that are founded on the same values—that is America and Europe—get on together," his chosen image hardly suggests the transatlantic solidarity that helped win the Cold War.

Shaken by Europe's failure to keep peace in the Balkans without U.S. leadership, British Prime Minister Tony Blair met with Chirac at St. Malo, France, in December 1998 and joined him in calling on the EU to develop "the capacity for autonomous action, backed up by credible military forces, the means to decide to use them, and a readiness to do so, in order to respond to international crises."

Yet Blair has rejected Chirac's idea of multipolarity, warning that if "the world breaks into different centers of power," these "would very quickly become rival centers of power," and "if you end up with two rival centers of power, you find a very, very difficult situation." By contrast, Blair has often spoken of his nation as a transatlantic "bridge," a medium of communication between America and Europe which allows both sides to inform and influence each other, and thus keep the alliance strong. This makes Blair the heir of his predecessors Churchill and Thatcher, as the main European advocate of what Garton Ash calls a "Euroatlanticist" foreign policy—a geopolitical grand strategy based on close alliance with the United States.

So the French are still Euro-Gaullists and the British still Euroatlanticists. You might well ask, "What else is new?" What's new is a cultural shift that has occurred in Europe, most crucially in Germany, since the fall of the Soviet Union.

Repudiating Germany's long and destructive history of militarism, the Federal Republic has always been reluctant to use force of arms. Until 1994, the nation's constitution was interpreted to prohibit the deployment of German forces outside NATO's borders, even as part of international peacekeeping operations. Yet as long as Russian troops remained poised to invade it, West Germany's leaders also recognized the need for a forceful deterrent, which inevitably meant a strong Atlantic alliance. Witness their willingness, in the face of strong protests from their own public, to let the U.S. deploy midrange missiles on German terrain in the 1980s.

Since the disappearance of the Soviet empire, the pacifist tendencies in German culture have grown stronger. In part, this has been an effect of the rise to power of the "'68" generation of radical activists, most notably Chancellor Gerhard Schröder and Foreign Minister Joschka Fischer. Another factor, according to Charles Hill, a veteran American diplomat who now teaches international relations at Yale University, was Germany's renewed sense of guilt for World War II and the Nazi genocide, stimulated by the bitter debate (known as the *Historikerstreit*) among German historians in the late 1980s. Whatever the deeper causes of this shift toward pacifism, it would not have been possible as long as Germany faced an obvious and imminent threat from Russia.

By eliminating the need for a U.S. security umbrella, the end of the Cold War exposed a values gap between Europe and America with regard to the use of military force, a gap which widened after 9/11. Although Europeans have suffered their share of terrorism, and almost all watched news of the World Trade Center and Pentagon attacks with horror and deep sympathy, they have been less widely sympathetic to America's military response. The doctrine of preemptive action, reaffirmed in the U.S. National Security Strategy released in 2002, has been especially controversial in Europe.

Nowhere is the values gap wider or more profound than between America and Germany. Today the Germans are Europe's foremost proponents of mediation and diplomacy as substitutes for military action, and of multilateralism as a means of containing the aggressive tendencies of nation-states. Such commitments would seem to have little in common with French "counterweight" strategy, which reeks of *Realpolitik* and the sort of nineteenth-century balance-of-power reasoning that the EU is supposed to have made obsolete. In fact, there is little enthusiasm in Germany (or for that matter in Europe) for turning the EU into a great power in the traditional sense. But pacifism *is* compatible with the idea of a united Europe reining in a unilateralist, bellicose America. Euro-Gaullism presented as the cause of multilateralism can thus draw German support. This is what happened in 2002, when Schröder won reelection on a platform denouncing U.S. policy toward Iraq; and again in 2003, when Germany joined France in opposing the American and British position on Iraq in the UN Security Council, on the grounds that, in the words of France's Foreign Minister Dominique de Villepin, "War is always an acknowledgment of failure."

Who Needs the Atlantic Alliance?

French and German leaders failed in 2003 to rally the EU against America's Iraq policy. Counting the eight post-Communist nations due to join in May 2004, all of which lined up behind Washington, a majority of member-state governments supported the U.S. position. Along with like-minded governments among the older member states, including Britain, Denmark, the Netherlands, and Spain (then still under the Euroatlanticist leadership of Prime Minister José María Aznar), the new members successfully pressed for the proposed European constitution to guarantee that EU security and defense policy must "respect" and "be compatible with" the obligations of NATO members under the North Atlantic Treaty—the first time that an EU treaty has made explicit reference to the Atlantic alliance in the form of NATO.[9] By bolstering the Euroatlanticist contingent within the EU, enlargement would seem to have confirmed the EU's commitment to the Atlantic alliance.

But the idea of Europe as a brake on reckless American power could still have a future in EU politics. As the Central and Eastern countries grow more economically and culturally integrated with the Western member states, and their memories of Communism fade, a stronger identification with the EU will no doubt compete with their loyalty to America. Britain, too, must balance its European commitments with ties to its old transatlantic ally. Even as good a friend of America as former External Relations Commissioner Chris Patten (now Lord Patten of Barnes, and Chancellor of the University of Oxford) has spoken of the EU as a "counterweight as well as a counterpart to the United States."[10] In Brussels, despite the pronounced Euroatlanticist tilt of the Barroso Commission, Euro-Gaullist talk resonates in the increasingly influential European Parliament.

Surveys by the German Marshall Fund since the Iraq war have shown a sharp drop in the numbers of Frenchmen, Germans, and—most strikingly—Britons favoring continued U.S. leadership in the world. In June 2004, a bare majority in Britain, 54 percent, still supported American leadership, but only 24 percent in France and 37 percent in Germany did so. There has been an equally impressive rise in support for turning the EU into a superpower, with 71 percent of Europeans favoring this goal in June 2004.[11]

Yet one of these same surveys also showed that only 22 percent of Europeans favored any rise in military spending, a proportion that is unlikely to increase unless and until an aging continent finds new ways to finance costly social services or modifies its commitment to the welfare state.[12] In the meantime, this leaves the EU with the option of acting as what founder Jean Monnet called a "civilian great power," relying on its clout in international organizations and other forms of soft power as well as its economic might to promote its interests and ideals.

If Europe should adopt a strategy of counterbalancing American power, it is fair to ask why America should care. After all, the sole superpower needs no permission from the UN Security Council, or the EU, or any other body to use military force. The U.S. can win wars on its own. Yet as the aftermath of the Iraq invasion has demonstrated, keeping the peace and rebuilding a conquered land are costly undertakings. The absence of French and German troops in Iraq has added to the burden of our overstretched forces there, as many as 40 percent of whom are reservists and National Guardsmen who never imagined serving such long tours of duty so far from home.

In a less concrete but no less consequential sense, the lack of UN Security Council or full NATO support for Operation Iraqi Freedom put a dent in America's global leadership, by lending credibility to the image of the U.S. as arrogantly unilateralist. Never mind that the U.S led a large multinational coalition to war in order to enforce a Security Council resolution and to defend the international state system of which the UN itself is the crowning formal expression.

Continued European criticism of this kind, by attacking the legiti-macy of our foreign policy, could further erode America's soft power in Europe and around the world.

During my tenure in Brussels, I saw how just a couple of coun-tries can stymie EU-NATO collaboration on a common security agenda. Since NATO is an intergovernmental organization that oper-ates by consensus—that is, with every member exercising a veto—a sustained Euro-Gaullist strategy on the part of a small minority could eventually hobble the Atlantic alliance. In that case, America would be unable to rely on NATO to relieve U.S. forces as it has done in Afghanistan.

On a practical level, an EU military could undermine the Atlantic alliance by competing for the same resources as NATO. Unless the training, equipment, and other technical requirements of EU forces are made fully compatible—or in military jargon, "interoperable"—with those of U.S. forces, as is the case with all NATO members today, countries that are members of both organizations will be forced to split their defense spending in order to meet distinct EU and NATO requirements, rendering their contributions less valuable to both. The EU's decision for or against interoperability will determine whether its common military identity is an asset or a liability to the EU's partnership with the United States.

Euro-Gaullism could impede transatlantic cooperation on the crucial intelligence and law enforcement fronts in the war against Islamist terrorism, by further politicizing issues such as extradition and sharing of evidence. We could expect more cases like that of Zacarias Moussaoui, the accused 9/11 conspirator to whose American prosecutors the German authorities refused to hand over evidence, lest Moussaoui's trial lead to a death sentence. Opposition to the death penalty is one of the defining elements in the EU's image as a guardian of human rights; and a Europe that defined itself in opposi-tion to the United States would no doubt discover other important differences in our standards of justice. Portugal, for instance, has already stopped extraditing prisoners who might face a sentence of life imprisonment.

Euro-Gaullism can be used to justify decisions driven by pri-marily commercial interests. France's President Chirac publicly

declared in 2001 that unless Europeans developed their own satellite navigation system, they would find themselves "first scientific
and technological vassals, then industrial and economic vassals" of
the United States. He might more accurately have said that a satellite navigation system outside of U.S. control would make it easier
for the European arms industry, the French in particular, to sell
sophisticated aircraft and guided munitions to other countries.

In their campaign to lift the EU's arms embargo on China,
France and Germany have not spoken openly of their desire to win
Chinese infrastructure contracts for their national industries. They
have spoken about Europe's supposed need to build an independent
strategic relationship with one of President Chirac's emerging "poles."
This, despite Beijing's continued belligerence toward Taiwan, which
the U.S. is committed to defend. An end to the embargo would
therefore increase the possibility of U.S. forces facing state-of-art
French Mirage jet fighters, German stealth submarines, and even
American-made precision-guided munitions in the Taiwan Strait.
China could also transfer such arms to enemies of America such as
Iran, as it has already done with U.S. missile and chemical weapons
technology. (Lifting the embargo would also come at a cost to the
EU's own soft power, since selling weapons to a country that contin-
ues to imprison and torture political dissidents would hardly bolster
Europe's image as a bastion of human rights.)

Yet for all the distress that Euro-Gaullism could cause the U.S.,
its effects on Europe would be no less dire. After all, the original purpose of the Atlantic alliance was to ensure the security of Europe.
Despite the end of Cold War, this is hardly a good to be taken for
granted, as demonstrated in the Balkans during the 1990s, not to
mention the many potential sources of instability along the EU's
periphery today: in the former Soviet Union, the Middle East, and
North Africa. The EU is now emerging as a defense and security
organization willing and able to act autonomously of the United
States. In time, Europe aims to guarantee its own security entirely
without U.S. help. But that day has not arrived.

Many Europeans understand this and would resist any common
foreign policy that put the alliance at risk. "If Europe sees its integration process as one directed against the United States, it will not

work because the result will be a split in Europe," said NATO's Secretary General Jaap de Hoop Scheffer in 2004. Euro-Gaullism would thus undermine the unity of the EU itself.

Although the U.S. no longer plays its Cold War leading role in Europe, it remains for many countries there a trusted outside guarantor of stability. For the Central and Eastern member states in particular, apprehensive about Russia or even (for Europeans have long memories) the possibility of a future German ascendancy, the Atlantic alliance is a kind of extra insurance policy.

The success of European integration continues to require, as it always has, a strong alliance with America. According to the economist Robert Mundell, the strength of the euro in particular depends on the Atlantic alliance, which fills the role of the great military power that has always stood behind any global currency.

Not only Europe and America stand to lose from a weakening of the Atlantic alliance; so does the rest of the world. The U.S. and the EU working together are a tremendous force for good: alleviating poverty, hunger, and disease; defending human rights; and increasing the possibilities for wealth creation through economic freedom. But if our cooperation breaks down, the losses will be incalculable, especially since these opportunities may not be ours for long.

China and India, whose populations will total over 2.5 billion by the year 2020, are expanding their military capabilities to match their economic growth rates (9.3 percent for China in 2003 and 5.2 percent for India, compared with 3 percent for the U.S. and 1 percent for the EU). Although these countries will not match Europe or America in terms of per capita income before the second half of this century, China and India will be global powers well before then, changing the geopolitical balance in unforeseeable ways.

As Lord Patten put it to me in late 2004, just before leaving his external relations duties at the Commission, the U.S. and the EU have two decades left to "shape the world" in the ways we deem best. After that, in his estimation, economic and demographic trends will force us to share that power with the two emerging Asian giants. His deadline sounds all too realistic to me. Meaning that now is the Atlantic moment, the moment of America and Europe. Will we seize it?

Notes

1. Schmitt, Burkard, "Defence Expenditure," February 2005, Paris: Institute for Strategic Studies European Union, pp. 2, 3, http://www .iss-eu.org/esdp/11-bsdef.pdf.

2. Harding, Gareth, "Analysis: Europe-America Defense Gap," United Press International, January 10, 2005, http://www.upi.com/view.cfm? StoryID=20050110-011653-8095r.

3. Nye, Joseph S., Jr., *Soft Power: The Means to Success in World Politics*, New York: PublicAffairs, 2004, p. 7.

4. These figures all refer to government donations. Private-sector American sources, far more significant than their counterparts in Europe, give about four times as much as the U.S. government, according to the U.S. Agency for International Development.

5. "The Image of Europe" (exhibition), co-created by Mark Leonard and Rem Koolhaas, Brussels, September 13–November 28, 2004.

6. National Intelligence Council, "Mapping the Global Future," Washington, D.C.: National Intelligence Council, p. 17.

7. Quoted in Peyrefitte, Alain, *C'était de Gaulle*, Paris: Fayard, 1994, p. 159.

8. Garton Ash, Timothy, *Free World: America, Europe, and the Surprising Future of the West*, New York: Random House, 2004.

9. Treaty Establishing a Constitution for Europe, Rome, October 29, 2004, Article I-43 (2), http://europa.eu.int/constitution/index_en.htm.

10. "Patten: Europe must have convincing evidence to join Iraq attack; dealing with terrorism should not be linked to dealing with Saddam," European Viewpoint, September 9, 2002, http://www.coeur.ws/european_ viewpoint/index.php?article=09-09-02.html.

11. German Marshall Fund of the United States and Compagnia di San Paolo, *Transatlantic Trends 2004*, "Key Findings Report," pp. 6, 16, http://www.transatlantictrends.org/. A later German Marshall Fund Poll, taken in late fall 2004, found that the percentages of French and Germans who found U.S. leadership undesirable had gone slightly down from June 2004, but were still much higher than before the Iraq war: more than twice as high in the case of France and over a third higher in the case of Germany. (Britain was not included in the later survey.) German Marshall Fund of the United States, "Post Election Study 2004," December 2004, p. 6, http:// www.gmfus.org/apps/gmf/gmfwebfinal.nsf/$UNIDviewAll/3B832E4C4B3BB 77685256F9F00700669?OpenDocument&K1E73ABE9.

12. *Transatlantic Trends 2004*, p. 8.

CHAPTER FIVE

The European Union as a Cultural Superpower

A PART FROM ITS intrinsic worth, European culture is one of the European Union's greatest assets in political and economic terms. Its prestige and appeal account for much of the EU's global influence and the receptivity of other states to its policies. And no one who has ever contemplated a vacation in Venice or bought a bottle of French Champagne will be surprised to hear that culture is a vital factor in European commerce.

But in another sense, Europe's rich variety of languages and traditions is a liability for the EU, hindering continental unity at the deepest level: that of identity. Common economic and political interests alone cannot persuade people that they belong to the same society. For that, they must believe that they share the same values; and culture is the domain in which values are formed and expressed. The EU's founding father Jean Monnet is said to have remarked late in life about his efforts to bring the continent together: "If I could begin again, I would begin with education and culture."

In all their cultural diversity, Europeans might find it easier to see themselves as one people by looking outwards, and defining themselves as what they are *not*, than by discerning and elaborating on the values that they hold in common. But whether the object of contrast be America or Islam, defining European identity in principally negative terms is an ultimately destructive strategy, threatening to cut Europe off from productive interaction with other cultures, to distort Europeans' understanding of their economic and geopolitical interests, and to impoverish European culture itself.

Culture as a Source of European Power

While the concepts of economic and geopolitical power are widely familiar, the idea of cultural power may require some explanation, starting with what I mean by culture. There are many definitions to choose from, but I like Joseph Nye's pithy characterization of culture as the "set of values and practices which create meaning for a society."[1] A bit more concretely, I think of it as referring to the broad area of human activity that includes (but is not limited to) religion, the arts, language, education, popular entertainment, sports, folk customs, manners, and food.

A discussion of culture properly starts with religion, because through most of history, religion has been culture's ultimate focus and highest expression. While Europeans themselves, especially in the Western countries, are today less observant than ever, their continent remains in many senses the center of Christianity, the world's most widely practiced faith.

Rome is of course headquarters for the Roman Catholic Church, and although a majority of cardinals today are non-European, the Vatican itself remains a largely Italian institution. Most of the patriarchs of the Orthodox churches reside in European countries, almost all of which are EU members or potential members. In the worldwide Anglican Communion, the Archbishop of Canterbury is first among equals, a respected arbiter of disputes between the other bishops. Some of the most influential theologians in the growing Evangelical movement live in Northern Europe, particularly in Britain and the Netherlands.

Europe is also home to almost all of Christianity's greatest shrines, which draw millions of pilgrims every year. Not only do these pilgrims pour money into the EU's economy; like tourists and business travelers, they give Europeans an invaluable opportunity to build good will with people from around the world.

One of the most conspicuous signs of Europe's religious heritage is its wealth of ecclesiastical art and architecture, mostly Christian but also Muslim and Jewish. Along with classical and secular masterpieces, these works make Europe the world's richest artistic treasury. No civilization has surpassed Europe's artistic achievements, and none has come close to preserving as many of its own.

Culture is an essential factor in Europe's tourist trade, one of the largest industries in several EU countries, including France, Italy, and Spain. Cultural attractions are especially important to the overseas market; for while many Germans and Britons flock to Mediterranean beaches, how many Americans or Japanese would come to Europe if there were no Parthenon or Louvre?

European culture draws the admiration of many who will never visit the continent. Despite a growing interest in non-Western art, the greatest museum collections in America and much of the world, like the repertoires of orchestras and opera companies, trace their origins overwhelmingly to Europe.

Language is another source of economic advantage and global political influence for Europe. Spanish is the world's fourth most widely spoken tongue, which makes most of Latin America a market for Spain's cultural production and a potential constituency for its international leadership. For similar reasons, France has long cultivated relations among the Francophone communities in Africa, Asia, and the Americas. Portugal, with only 10.5 million people and one of the lowest GDPs in Western Europe, exerts an influence out of proportion to its size owing to linguistic ties with Brazil, a nation of 184 million, as well as several African countries. Not to mention English—a European tongue, lest we Americans forget—which is now the de facto international language of the EU as well as the world.

In education, several Northern European countries set global standards of excellence for elementary and secondary schools. Finnish high school students in particular have been judged the world's second most proficient in mathematics (after their counterparts in Hong Kong).[2] Britain's Oxford and Cambridge are world-class research universities, and in recent years, Europe's output of published scientific research has exceeded America's. European universities in general remain popular destinations for American students taking a semester or year abroad, a practice which builds respect and affinity for Europe in the rising generation of professionals and academics.

One need not be conscious of European culture to fall under its sway. Britain's pop music industry has global reach, and Europe sets international trends in other forms of entertainment. "Reality television" is largely the creation of Dutch entrepreneur John de Mol, producer of *Big Brother* and *Fear Factor*. European teams are reliably among the very best in European football, the world's most popular sport (and one in which the U.S. presence is negligible). In design and fashion, all the way down the price range from Bulgari jewelry to Ikea flat-packed furniture, European companies are internationally competitive or dominant. There are hundreds of products, such as Spanish sherry, French Bordeaux, Normandy Camembert, and Parma ham, that connoisseurs around the world will not consider buying unless they originate in a particular European region.

The benefits to Europe in all these fields are more than economic. Shaping taste means shaping values, and cultural influence can translate into political influence, even through something as seemingly apolitical as food. The Slow Food movement started in Italy in 1986, dedicated to defending the "right to taste," and now has over 80,000 members. Fewer than 15,000 of these are in the U.S., but their high socioeconomic profile makes them disproportionately influential. Their celebration of fresh, locally made food products appeals to the same Americans who buy organic foods, a market of over $11 billion. This trend has natural implications for the public's views on environmental policies and agricultural subsidies. It could encourage a shift in American dining habits, back toward longer meals at home, which would in turn mean changed attitudes toward work and leisure, with all the economic and political consequences *those* would imply. But even if it never has such far-reaching effects, Slow Food is already moving one area of American life in the direction of Europe.

Culture as a Source of European Identity

Though European culture exerts a powerful attraction on the rest of the world, it has been far less effective at drawing together the diverse nations of the EU. To put it another way, whereas Europe's economic integration is in many respects nearly complete and its political integration well underway, the continent's cultural integration has barely begun.

In fact, it would be more accurate to refer to Europe's cultural *re-*integration. Cultural links among the European nations are complex and deeply layered, the fruit of millennia of interaction through conquest, trade, proselytizing, and migration. But more recent political and social trends have largely obliterated these historical ties.

Religion

Since at least as far back as the year 800, when Pope Leo III crowned Charlemagne the first emperor of the West, Europe has been synonymous with Christendom. The founding fathers of the European Union were all practicing Roman Catholics; and the Vatican has considered at least one of them, the French Prime Minister Robert Schuman (1886–1963), a serious candidate for beatification, one step from sainthood. The largest group in the European Parliament today is a coalition of "Christian Democrats," political parties from across the continent originally united by their common religious inspiration.

Yet despite the efforts of several Roman Catholic nations led by Italy and Poland, the 2004 constitutional treaty included no explicit reference to Europe's Christian heritage. The fiercest opposition to such a reference came from France, a state whose strict policy of secularism (*laïcité*) is a century-old legacy of its struggle against the once-formidable political power of the Catholic Church. In late 2004, the European Parliament's rejection of an Italian commissioner-designate who had espoused Catholic doctrine on sexuality during his confirmation hearings convinced many of the EU's institutional hostility to Christianity.

Whatever the attitudes in Brussels, the European public today is hardly embracing faith. Only 21 percent of Europeans tell pollsters that religion is "very important" to them, compared with 59 percent of Americans; and only 15 percent of Europeans say that they attend a place of worship once a week, whereas the U.S. figure is 44 percent. This leads many commentators to characterize Europe as a "post-Christian society." But one learned observer has made the intriguing suggestion that Europe today may be a *pre*-Christian society. According to Alister McGrath, a professor of historical theology at the University of Oxford, Eastern Europe is disillusioned with atheism after decades under Communism, and Western European culture is in a "postmodern" phase marked by increasing interest in spirituality, all of which could make the continent fertile ground for a revival of religious faith.[3]

Historically, religion has brought Europe together in a profoundly negative sense through its persecution of minority faiths, especially Judaism; and some today see a source of unity in the repudiation of that injustice. The epic suffering of European Jewry over the centuries—which makes Jews' contribution to every branch of European culture all the more glorious an achievement—culminated in the Nazi genocide during World War II. That war was the cataclysm that moved the founders of the EU to start the process of European integration. Therefore, according to Bronislaw Geremek, a Polish medieval historian and member of the European Parliament, "it should be said that the Holocaust helped to create the European Union. It was the answer to the totalitarian ideology created on European soil, such as Auschwitz."[4]

Alas, European anti-Semitism today is not merely a subject for historians. In recent years, attacks on synagogues, Jewish schools, and cemeteries in Europe have grown markedly more frequent, most notably in France, which has the largest number of Jews in the EU, over 500,000 out of a population of 60 million. Discussing this problem at a dinner given by the American Jewish Committee in Brussels in February 2004, I expressed my view that things had not been so bad since the 1930s. The following day, press reports misquoted me as having said that the situation was *as* bad as during the Nazi era, something which I would never have claimed, and which is thankfully far from the case.

European reaction to my putative statement was predictably sensitive, especially since the EU had recently been criticized for shelving an official report which attributed many anti-Jewish incidents to

Muslim immigrants. Fortunately, the Commission addressed the issue in a seminar later that month in Brussels and published a new report on anti-Semitism that spring. Yet tensions over this matter, and generally over relations with the continent's growing Muslim population (see below), suggest that for the foreseeable future, religion will be a divisive rather than unifying force in the EU.

Arts and Sciences

Europe's patrimony of art, music, literature, philosophy, science, and scholarship is the product of centuries of international exchange and cross-fertilization, a legacy to which all the continent may lay claim. The most important artistic and intellectual movements in European history—including Scholasticism, the Renaissance, and the Enlightenment—transcended national boundaries as we know them today. Shakespeare's works are no more exclusively English than Beethoven's are exclusively German; both men drew and built on the achievements of a common civilization. Unfortunately, as a result of the nationalism which dominated European politics in the nineteenth and early twentieth centuries, most Europeans now view the great works and minds of the past as the property of particular nation-states.

A graphic illustration of this attitude of separate ownership is found in the history of European money. A number of currencies in the EU once carried portraits of artists, scientists, and other thinkers as emblems of patriotic pride; but proposals to put such images on euro banknotes failed, for fear of offending national sentiment in any of the twelve countries using the common currency. While the final designs for euro bills did feature architectural illustrations, of bridges, doors, and windows belonging to periods from classical antiquity to the twentieth century, the designer made sure—in at least one case, by deliberately blurring the image—that they could not be identified with structures in any particular country. The EU is still a long way from the vision of Salvador de Madariaga, the Spanish diplomat and founder of the College of Europe, who wrote, "when Spaniards say 'our Chartres,' Englishmen 'our Cracow,' Italians 'our Copenhagen,' when Germans say 'our Bruges.' . . . Then will Europe live."

Education

Europe's universities were once nexuses in an international cultural network, and the greatest of all—such as Paris, Oxford, Salamanca, and Bologna in the High Middle Ages—were truly pan-European institutions. More recently, the EU has tried to use higher education to cultivate a common European identity: the ERASMUS exchange program has sent more than a million European undergraduates to study for up to one academic year in a different European country. The French movie *The Spanish Apartment* (2002) portrays a multi-national group of such students forming a jolly "Euro pudding" in an apartment in Barcelona.

During my tenure as ambassador to the EU, I visited some twenty universities across the continent, from Turkey to Britain. At every school I visited, there was one question I always asked: how many of the students regarded themselves as Europeans first, and only secondarily as citizens of their home countries? Often more than half the class would raise their hands. At the College of Europe in Bruges, Belgium, the proportion was over two-thirds (which is only fitting for an institution that prepares its multinational student body to work at the Commission and other EU institutions). Yet I was also struck by how many young people described themselves as enthusiastically European even while holding strong national identities.

Unfortunately, many of the administrators and instructors at European universities are less cosmopolitan than their students. Except in Britain and Ireland, where institutions choose their academic staff through international competitions, higher education is one of the EU's most heavily protected industries. In the worst cases, such as Spain and Italy, academics commonly spend their entire careers, from undergraduate enrollment to tenured professorship, at the same university. Scholars continually decry the intellectual sterility that such inbreeding produces, but efforts at reform have thus far yielded modest results.[5] As much as academics may chafe to hear their profession described in commercial terms, Europe needs a single market in higher education.

Language

The most obvious barrier to international education is language. A university operating in a tongue spoken only locally, such as Finnish, Catalan, or Italian, will find it practically impossible to attract foreign teachers or students. To compete internationally, a rising number of European universities are therefore offering degree programs taught in English, opening themselves up to the rest of Europe and the world.

This trend could vastly enhance the EU as a center of research, especially since the U.S. has made it harder in the wake of 9/11 for foreigners to come and study here. In 2004, major U.S. graduate schools reported that new foreign enrollments were down for the third straight year, which commentators attributed above all to difficulties in obtaining student visas. Meanwhile, Britain has seen a rise in non-European enrollments, and that benefit could spread to other European countries with universities that teach in English.[6] Graduate students are essential for staffing research teams in engineering and science. And because the largest numbers of international graduate students today come from China and India, attracting more of them will enhance the EU's soft power by building ties with future elites in those rising Asian powers.

English is already the lingua franca of European business, as reflected in the growing numbers of European business schools offering MBA programs in that language. Even more remarkably, since the EU's enlargement to twenty-five nation-states in 2004, English has also become the de facto common language of pan-European institutions. The EU has twenty official languages, which are sometimes in use all at once, such as at plenary sessions and committee hearings of the European Parliament. But when members of Parliament from different countries mingle in the hallways, they usually talk to each other in English.

Though this development was inevitable—how else is a Lithuanian going to address a Spaniard, or a Cypriot a Pole?—it has nonetheless inspired resistance and resentment, particularly in France. Proud of their nation's prominent role in the history of European integration, the French have tried to preserve their language's currency within the EU institutions, for instance by offering free lessons to Commission officials from the newest member states. The French are also vigilant about protecting their tongue from infection with English words and phrases—for example, by insisting that government employees use the term *courriel* instead of the universal standard "e-mail." With 130 million speakers worldwide, French is presumably less threatened by English than is Finnish, which has only 6 million speakers; yet Finnish officials speak English eagerly. Fears that using the language of Shakespeare will somehow lead to "Anglo-Saxon" domination of the EU have no historical basis. After all, the lingua franca of the Roman Empire was Greek, not Latin, yet it was the Romans who ran the show.

Popular Culture

America's encroachment on European culture is most obvious in the area of popular entertainment, especially films. The only images you are sure to find on screens from Helsinki to Seville are the faces of Hollywood stars. Not surprisingly, this state of affairs especially disturbs the French. "There is a tendency towards a prevailing Anglo-Saxon culture which eclipses the others," President Jacques Chirac warned students in Hanoi in October 2004, while visiting Vietnam on a trade-promotion tour. "If we accepted our American friends' ideas, there would quite quickly be only one form of cultural expression, and all the others would be stifled to the sole benefit of American culture."

France's defense against this peril is the so-called "cultural exception" to free trade, meaning that films, television, music, and other cultural production are not subject to EU rules against state subsidies and import quotas. Defenders of such protectionism argue that it preserves Europe's cultural diversity. Certainly it is responsible for many films that would never otherwise have been made. But subsidies also reduce a filmmaker's incentive to attract an audience, with results that are often unwatchable. Even in France, half the total box-office receipts typically go to Hollywood movies. That's why some EU nations such as Italy are requiring filmmakers to raise more of their financing commercially, and making it easier for studios to produce subsidized films in English, as ways of rendering their national movie industries more internationally competitive.

The one major expression of culture in which all EU nations take part together, and with great enthusiasm, is European football. Competition at the higher levels is pan-European, and fans closely track the statistics in other national leagues. The most devoted aficionados fly across the continent to watch key matches. Could sports be the basis on which to build a common European identity? Maybe so, but rowdy spectators increasingly use soccer games as a chance to flaunt, sometimes violently, the nationalism which integration has removed from European civic life. For now, it seems, sports can bring Europeans together, but not necessarily in harmony.

Europe as Not-America

Recent years have brought increasing anxiety within the EU over the question: "What is Europe?" This anxiety has grown especially acute with the accession of the ten newest members, eight of them Central and Eastern countries with Communist backgrounds, which have transformed the union into a far more heterogeneous group than before.

Valéry Giscard d'Estaing, the former French president who presided over the drafting of the 2004 constitutional treaty, addressed this problem in an article published in *The Financial Times* in November 2004. Considering the record low turnout of voters in that year's elections for the European Parliament, Giscard concluded that "Europeans need to strengthen their identity. No 'European patriotism' can exist until European citizens realize that they belong to a single entity."[7]

In attempting to offer a "clearer definition of the foundations of this entity," Giscard invoked the "cultural contributions of ancient Greece and Rome, the religious heritage pervading European life, the creative enthusiasm of the Renaissance, the philosophy of the Age of the Enlightenment and the contributions of rational and scientific thought." These, he wrote, are "the foundations of our identity, so vital to the cohesion of the European Union today."

Yet as Giscard acknowledged, and as I have explained above, this glorious heritage has not been enough to convince European citizens "that they belong to a single entity." As the EU has grown larger and more integrated in recent years, opinion surveys show that Europeans have grown more likely to identify exclusively with their nationality than with Europe as a whole.[8] Perhaps with time, as Europeans deal increasingly with each other in a single market and grow used to living with each other in a common polity, they will rediscover their shared cultural past. Making sure that they do so will fall in the end to the schools and universities, and the job will be neither easy nor quick.

But just because Europeans are not yet conscious of being a single people, does this mean that they are not? Their shared heritage has presumably endowed them with certain common values, even if they do not realize it. If so, these must be the values that define European society.

More than one thinker in recent years has tried to define Europe in such terms. One of the most celebrated attempts has been by the German philosopher Jürgen Habermas, who in May 2003 published an article, also signed by the late French philosopher Jacques Derrida, in the *Frankfurter Allgemeine Zeitung* newspaper. In this article, Habermas suggests six values as possible elements of a "European identity": the "social privatization of faith," or secularism; greater confidence in government than in the free market; skepticism about the benefits of progress (presumably expressed through support for strict environmental regulation); an egalitarian social ethos; "sensitivity to injuries to personal and bodily integrity," expressed through opposition to the death penalty; and support for "mutual limitation of sovereignty" of nation-states, or what we would call multilateralism.[9]

Habermas locates the roots of these values in European history, but in context it is clear that he has chosen them to draw a contrast between Europe and America. The article's main title is "February 15, or What Binds Europeans Together," the date in question being that of large protests across Europe against the looming Iraq war in 2003. These protests, Habermas writes, "may well, in hindsight, go down in history as a sign of the birth of a European public sphere." In other words, a common European identity, defined in contrast to American values, has finally emerged in response to an assertion of American power.

Here is a particularly systematic expression of a concept which Timothy Garton Ash calls "Europe as Not-America," a cultural corollary to the geopolitical strategy of Euro-Gaullism.[10] The idea has become increasingly common in the words of European politicians, journalists, and other commentators since the controversial run-up to the Second Gulf War, but its origins lie farther back.

Sociology and common experience teach us that groups tend to define themselves by distinction from other groups with which they are in close contact. Scotsmen distinguish themselves from Englishmen, Britons from Continental Europeans, and so on. For the first four decades of European integration, if the Western nations defined themselves collectively, it was as part of the West (or the "Free World") against the common foe of Soviet Communism, right on the other side of the Iron Curtain. With the disappearance of that foe at the start of the 1990s, just as European integration was beginning to occur on the political level, there arose the temptation to define the EU in opposition to the only power worthy of such a comparison, the United States.

As the EU matures as a polity, I believe it will outgrow any negatively determined conception of itself. In the meantime, the all-too-popular idea of Europe as Not-America undermines the relationship between the U.S. and the EU and gives a distorted image of Europe's own character.

Defining European identity in this way means exaggerating or overemphasizing the differences in values between Europe and America. Take another look at Habermas's list. With the partial exception of opposition to the death penalty, every item on it is a staple of successful political platforms throughout so-called blue-state America, the base of support for Democratic presidential candidates in the last two elections. In 2004, Senator John F. Kerry, with his repeated calls for closer consultation with "our allies" (i.e., the Europeans), to say nothing of his French relatives and fluency in the language, was widely seen as a sort of honorary European—not least within the EU, where surveys showed a wide majority supporting his election. That Kerry lost the race does not undo the fact that 48 percent of American voters chose the candidate espousing ostensibly European values.

This is not to suggest, as many in the press would have it, that Democrats are somehow in a better position to deal with Europe than Republicans are. Quite the contrary. As the party of enterprise, the GOP is by far the better steward of America's enormous trade and investment relationship with Europe, which is the fundamental stabilizing factor in transatlantic relations generally. On the other hand, the surest recipe for deep and lasting conflict between the U.S. and the EU would be for Washington to enact the protectionist policies still all too popular on the Democratic side of the aisle.

Nor are conservative American values necessarily alien to Europe. Like the U.S., the EU has its "red" and "blue" constituencies, and all the subtler shades that such a division fails to represent. Mixing religion and politics is far more acceptable in some EU countries, such as Italy and Spain, than in France. The Irish and the Poles attend weekly religious services in higher proportions (56 percent and 54 percent, respectively) than Americans (44 percent).[11] The new post-Communist member states are forceful advocates for economic liberalization and the preservation of national sovereignty within the EU. Polls show that capital punishment, though anathema to European elites and illegal throughout the EU, is popular in several European nations.[12]

Even if we accept that prevailing values in the U.S. and the EU differ along the lines that Habermas draws, concentrating on those differences means underrating the more important moral foundation that our societies share. Habermas himself sums up our common ethical grounding as the "Western form of spirit, rooted in the Judeo-Christian tradition," which is the basis for our shared belief in individual rights and responsibilities and ultimately for our institutions of liberal and democratic government. It is vital to remember that these institutions and values are far from universally espoused. Just as during World War II and the Cold War, they are under siege again today, most immediately by Islamist terrorists and the regimes that support them. Defending these values must remain our common priority. As the political scientist Simon Serfaty has argued, America and Europe constitute a community of interests and values, which we must translate into a community of action.[13]

There is no reason why Europeans and Americans cannot debate and disagree, as different political constituencies do in the U.S., while recognizing and reaffirming the overarching framework of Western civilization that contains us all. Polemics over our differences encourage the simplistic view, on both sides of the ocean, that complex political choices break down between mutually exclusive "American" and "European" alternatives. In such a view, economic globalization is a force for Americanization, and therefore a threat to the European way of life. Or multilateral negotiation through international organizations is a European plot to ensnare American power, and necessarily a menace to our security.

The idea of Europe as Not-America is destructive not merely of transatlantic harmony but of European integration itself. Since it is bound to alienate the many in Europe who view the U.S. with admiration and affection, the idea breeds internal division rather than unity. And by focusing on our differences rather than our deeper commonalities, it takes for granted, and thus diminishes, those Western values that truly bind Europeans together.

Europe as Not-Islam

In recent years, another negatively based concept of European identity has drawn increasing support from European political and cultural leaders. Although this idea might seem to be virtually the opposite of Europe as Not-America, it is similarly misguided, and its potential effects are hardly less destructive. I call it Europe as Not-Islam.

Christian Europe's intimate, rich, and frequently violent relationship with the Muslim world stretches back thirteen centuries, but at the beginning of European integration half a century ago, interaction between the two civilizations was negligible. This is no longer the case, for two major reasons: the increasing plausibility of Turkey's candidacy for EU membership and the growing number of Muslims within the EU.

Turkey first signed an association agreement with the European Economic Community, predecessor of the EU, in 1963 and has sought full membership ever since. It formally applied in 1987 but was rejected two years later, largely on account of its authoritarian political system, which for several years had taken the form of outright military rule, as well as its treatment of the country's Kurdish minority. Since 1989, Turkey has enacted extensive measures to bring it into line with European norms regarding human rights, the death penalty, the use of torture, the rights of women and ethnic minorities, and the primacy of civilian rule, among other issues. These reforms accelerated dramatically after 2002 under Prime Minister Recep Tayyip Erdogan, who made membership in the EU a top priority of his government.

On December 17, 2004, after some highly contentious preliminary talks, the EU member states announced that formal negotiations over Turkey's membership would begin the following October. Yet public opinion surveys at the time showed that large numbers in several EU member states, including Austria, France, and Germany, were opposed to admitting Turkey. Politicians in a number of countries, including Germany and the Netherlands, openly voiced their opposition. Even EU leaders stressed that negotiations would last many years, with no guarantee of success. Opposition to Turkey's accession was a major factor in the rejection by French and (especially) Dutch voters of the proposed EU constitution. Prime Minister Erdogan and many of his countrymen have complained, with some justice, of being judged by a different standard than other candidates past and present.

Some have objected to Turkey's accession on the grounds that it is poor. Yet its per capita GDP is only slightly lower than that of Romania or Bulgaria, which are both slated to join in 2007. Moreover, Turkey's GDP is probably half again as high as the official figure, owing to activities in the "shadow economy." Given the reductions that the EU must soon make in agricultural subsidies and development assistance to its current members, Turkey would not be a financial burden on the rest.

Others have opposed Turkey on the even less convincing grounds of geography, forgetting that EU member state Cyprus lies 200 miles to the east of Istanbul.

The real difficulty with Turkish membership is clearly religion. Although its government and public life have been strictly secular since the regime established by Kemal Ataturk (1881–1938), the nation's population of 69 million today is 99.8 percent Muslim. Turkey would be not just the first EU member state with a non-

Christian majority; given demographic trends, within twenty years it would be the most populous member state of all.

Since the EU is a secular organization, most opponents of Turkish membership decline to cite religion as an impediment, pointing instead to differences in European and Turkish "culture." This is mere wordplay. If Turkey today is as secular, modern, and committed to the Western values of democracy and human rights as its leaders claim, other cultural differences ought not bar economic and political union with the rest of Europe. But if the problem is Turkey's cultural *heritage*, which is of course inseparable from Islam, then the problem is religion after all.

The fiercest defenders of secularism oppose Turkish membership as strongly as do the champions of Europe's Christian identity. Both Pope Benedict XVI and former French President Giscard, who differed over whether the constitutional treaty should refer to Europe's Christian heritage, emphatically agree that Turkey is disqualified from EU membership on the grounds of "culture." Secularists, especially in France, worry that the Islamist movement which helped bring the current Turkish government to power will, despite Prime Minister Erdogan's assurances to the contrary, eventually transgress barriers between church and state. (At least one secularist is less fastidious in private about the distinction between culture and religion. Lunching with Giscard in Brussels in March 2002, I was startled to hear him state that the EU could never accept a Muslim country as large as Turkey, since Europe is "essentially a Christian society.")[14]

Islamism, a political ideology which calls for the state to submit to religious authority, and which in recent years has inspired the most horrific terrorism, is undoubtedly a serious concern with regard to Turkish accession. Imposing EU norms of human rights would probably remove one of Turkey's major brakes on extremism, by ending its government's power to appoint and supervise religious leaders. Yet several EU states including Germany and Britain enforce strict limits on speech and expression in order to prevent social strife, and similar laws could presumably apply in Turkey.

What is vital is that EU leaders approach such problems constructively, and in cooperation with Turkish leaders, rather than use the problems as excuses to derail Turkey's accession. With its youthful, hardworking population, powerful military, and eagerness to join the West, Turkey would be a priceless asset to the EU in demographic, economic, and geopolitical terms. Bringing this NATO member more fully into Europe's defense structure would make the region more secure, as should be clear from the enthusiastic support that its ancient enemy Greece now shows for Turkey's admission. Greece wants Turkey imbedded in the multilateral structure of a united Europe, for much the same reason that France wanted this of Germany half a century ago.

During my visits to Turkey in late 2004, the politicians, business people, and intellectuals I met all stressed to me that their nation's characteristic approach to Islam, unlike the traditions in neighboring lands, is moderate and compatible with Western values. All who seek the spread of those values should draw inspiration from the prospect of a democratic Muslim state fully integrated into Europe. We should also find the contrary prospect—of a dynamic and modernizing Muslim nation spurned at the door to the West—intolerably demoralizing.

Islam as a European Religion

If the goal is keeping Islam out of Europe, closing the door to Turkey would be not merely demoralizing but futile. The EU's Muslim population, already 15 million, is bound to grow ever more quickly in coming years owing to immigration and fertility rates far above the European average.

When European integration began more than half a century ago, the number of Muslims in Western Europe was trivial. The so-called "economic miracle" (*Wirtschaftswunder*) of Germany's postwar reconstruction led to a labor shortage, which grew much worse after 1961 when the Berlin Wall cut off West Germany's supply of workers from the east. Beginning in the mid-1950s, the Federal Republic recruited millions of foreign "guest workers" (*Gastarbeiter*), first from poorer Western European countries such as Italy and Spain, later from Muslim countries including Turkey and Morocco. Other European countries were rebuilt with the labor of Muslim immigrants: Pakistanis in Britain, North Africans in France, and Turks and Moroccans in the Netherlands.

European societies took various approaches to the novel challenge of absorbing different ethnic groups. France required newcomers to assimilate to its strong national culture and secularist tradition. Britain, by contrast, encouraged immigrant communities to retain the customs and social structures of their home countries. The latter approach, part of what came to be called multiculturalism, involved the use of ethnic leaders, including religious figures, as intermediaries between immigrant communities and the state. The Netherlands adopted a version of this policy, and to some extent so did Germany.

Beginning in the 1960s, the growth of Muslim and other non-white immigrant communities led to increasing social tensions in many European countries, including the emergence of openly racist political parties such as the National Fronts in France and Britain. However, such movements remained on the extreme fringes of the right—in Germany, they were effectively suppressed by that country's strict hate speech laws—and opposition to immigration generally remained beyond the pale of respectable opinion.

In the 1990s, relations between Muslims and the majority population in Europe grew ever more tense. Urban and suburban ghettos of largely unemployed Muslim immigrants and their offspring became a widely acknowledged social crisis. (Europe's rigidly regulated labor markets exacerbated the problem, by limiting the number of low-paying, entry-level jobs of the kind often taken by new arrivals to the United States.) The French government clashed with Muslim communities over the right of girls to wear traditional headscarves in state schools, a practice which the French parliament finally banned in 2004 (along with all other classroom displays of "ostensible religious symbols" such as crucifixes or stars of David) on the principle of *laïcité*. Religiously based political movements antagonistic to the values of modern European society increasingly raised concern. Islamist leaders in several EU countries openly preached revolution and violence, and some Muslim houses of worship were found to be linked with terrorist networks.

The 9/11 attacks, which were planned in Hamburg, Germany, and several other European cities, heightened these worries; and the Madrid bombings of March 11, 2004, intensified them. It is no coincidence that racist parties have made alarming gains in recent years.

Jean-Marie Le Pen of the National Front outpolled the Socialist Prime Minister Lionel Jospin to win second place in France's 2002 presidential elections, forcing a runoff with President Chirac. Almost as shocking, in September 2004 an overtly neo-Nazi party won 9.2 percent of the popular vote, and 12 out of 120 seats in the state legislature, in the German state of Saxony.

Equally unexpected has been the rise of so-called "postmodern populism," exemplified by the writers Oriana Fallaci and Michel Houellebecq and the slain Dutch politician Pim Fortuyn, who have fiercely criticized Islam and Muslim immigrant communities for their intolerance of homosexuality and their subordination of women. In the same spirit, the Dutch movie director Theo van Gogh, great-grandnephew of the Postimpressionist painter, made a provocative short film in collaboration with a Somali-born Dutch politician to protest the condition of women in Islamic society. His murder in November 2004, apparently by an Islamist militant of Moroccan origin, and the death threats to his collaborator and several government officials after the suspect's arrest, shocked the famously tolerant and multicultural Netherlands. Later that month, a prominent member of the Dutch parliament, Geert Wilders, publicly called for an end to non-Western immigration and the closing of radical mosques.

Undoubtedly, EU nations must improve their approaches to the integration of Muslim immigrants. France's Interior Minister Nicolas Sarkozy, an expected candidate for president in 2007, has called for rethinking his nation's secularist tradition, raising the possibility of government stipends for moderate Muslim preachers and affirmative action programs to reduce Muslim unemployment. On the other hand, Germany's Christian Democratic opposition leader Angela Merkel has pronounced multiculturalism a failure and affirmed the importance of a "leading culture" to which newcomers must assimilate. The Netherlands and Denmark already require immigrants to take classes in the local language and culture as a condition of their residence permits.

One option that EU leaders do not have is holding back the flow of Muslim immigrants. If present demographic trends continue, 60 percent of the EU will be over sixty-five years old by the middle of the century.[15] An aging Europe is going to need many millions more foreign-born workers to pay its retirees' pensions and care physically for the old themselves; and a majority of these immigrants will come from nearby countries in North Africa and the Middle East. If not admitted legally, they will come in anyway. Europe's economic needs and the porous nature of its borders, especially in the Mediterranean, make that a certainty.

While European populations shrink, Muslim nations are growing. The fertility rate is 4.11 children per woman in Saudia Arabia, 2.95 in Egypt, and 2.81 in Morocco compared with 1.48 in the EU. Even within Europe, Muslims have more children than the population at large. France's relatively high fertility rate of 1.85 is due largely to the Muslims already there: at least 5 million, and possibly as many as 8 million, out of a population of 60 million.

So the Muslim population of the EU will keep growing, through birth and immigration if not through enlargement of the Union's membership. The challenge will be to make these people fully part of European society. Will this mean, in spite of all multiculturalist qualms, persuading them to adopt Western civic values? While ordinary Europeans may despair of this when they see women in veils or headscarves, or hear the poisonous rhetoric of radical imams, a close observer of the scene finds cause for hope—not only for Muslim immigrants in Europe, but for Muslim civilization as a whole. In the words of Gilles Kepel, the French political scientist and Middle East expert:

> In Westminster, the European Parliament, the Bundestag, and in regional and municipal councils throughout Western Europe, the democratic political system that emerged from the European enlightenment is starting to absorb men and women born in a Muslim tradition, for the first time in history. . . . [This] opens the possibility that a new generation of Muslim thinkers will emerge— men and women with a universalist perspective, freed from the straitjacket of authoritarianism and corruption, emancipated from subservience toward their rulers and from the rage of a rebellion that endorses jihad, excommunication, and violence. . . . [T]he Islamists themselves, once they are actors in the European political arena, find their own rigid principles giving way to the compromises of democracy. . . . [T]hese young men and women will

present a new face of Islam—reconciled with modernity—to the larger world.[16]

In meeting the challenge posed by Islam on its own soil, Europe could thus become a cradle of Islamic democracy. That would be an achievement of incalculable benefit to the freedom, security, and prosperity of all nations—an achievement worthy of a cultural super-power. Yet the EU should also join with the U.S. to promote democracy in Iraq, Lebanon, and Iran, and throughout the Muslim world. These complementary missions are among the most urgent awaiting the emergence of a transatlantic community of action, founded on our deeply rooted community of interests and values.

Notes

1. Nye, p. 11.
2. "First Results from PISA 2003: Executive Summary," Paris: OECD, 2004, p. 9, http://www.pisa.oecd.org/dataoecd/1/63/34002454.pdf.
3. Ford, Peter, "What place for God in Europe?" *The Christian Science Monitor*, February 22, 2005; McGrath, Alister, "The incoming sea of faith," *The Spectator*, September 18, 2004, pp. 12, 13.
4. Dempsey, Judy, "Auschwitz adds to U.S.-EU friction," *The International Herald Tribune*, January 26, 2005.
5. Navarro, Arcadio, and Ana Rivero, "High Rate of Inbreeding in Spanish Universities," *Nature* 410 (2001), p. 14.
6. Bollag, Burton, "Enrollment of Foreign Students Drops in U.S.," *The Chronicle of Higher Education*, November 19, 2004.
7. Giscard, Valéry, "A better European bridge to Turkey," *The Financial Times*, November 25, 2004.
8. *Eurobarometer Spring 2004: Public Opinion in the European Union*, Joint Full Report of Eurobarometer 61 and CC Eurobarometer 2004.1, The European Commission: Brussels, 2004, p. B.95. http://europa.eu.int/comm/public_opinion/archives/eb/eb61/eb61_en.pdf.
9. Habermas, Jürgen, and Jacques Derrida, "February 15, or What Binds Europeans Together: A Plea for a Common Foreign Policy, Beginning in the Core of Europe," translated by Max Pensky, *Constellations*, 10: 3 (2003), pp. 291–297. (The article originally appeared in the *Frankfurter Allgemeine Zeitung*, 31 May 2003.)

10. Garton Ash, Timothy, *Free World: America, Europe, and the Surprising Future of the West*, New York: Random House, 2004, chapter 2, pp. 46–83.

11. Ford.

12. Opinion surveys have shown that up to three quarters of Britons, and roughly half of Italians and Swedes, support the return of the death penalty. Marshall, Joshua Micah, "Death in Venice," *The New Republic*, July 31, 2000.

13. See, for example, Simon Serfaty, *The Vital Partnership: Power and Order, America and Europe Beyond Iraq*, Lanham, Md.: Rowman & Littlefield, 2005.

14. The Pope's views on Turkey's accession (expressed in 2004, when he was still a cardinal) were taken seriously, even though the Vatican is not an EU member state, because an estimated 270 million of the EU's 458 million citizens profess to be Roman Catholics.

15. "Half a Billion Americans?" *The Economist*, August 22, 2002. The prediction was made for an EU of fifteen member states, but the situation has not improved with enlargement, since the addition of ten members in May 2004 actually lowered the average EU fertility rate to 1.46 children per woman from 1.47. *Fertility and Family Issues in an Enlarged Europe*, Dublin: European Foundation for the Improvement of Living and Working Conditions, 2004, p. 9, http://www.eurofound.eu.int/publications/files/EF03115EN.pdf.

16. Kepel, Gilles, *The War for Muslim Minds: Islam and the West*, translated by Pascale Ghazaleh, Cambridge and London: Belknap-Harvard, 2004, pp. 294, 295.

———— ⌁ ————

CHAPTER SIX

Dealing with the
European Union

"**I**F I WANT to reach Europe, whom do I call?"

This question, famously attributed to former Secretary of State Henry A. Kissinger, is now even more relevant—and harder to answer—than when he supposedly asked it three decades ago. Dealing with the European Union is unlike dealing with any other foreign power in history. In the EU, power is divided among twenty-five member states as well as the European institutions, along lines that vary widely depending on the area of law or policy in question and which are not always clear to the authorities themselves. As if that weren't complicated enough, these internal power relationships are not static but continually shifting, since the EU is an organization still very much under construction.

The labyrinthine complexity, and sometimes sheer confusion, of the EU can be no excuse for the U.S. to dismiss or ignore it. As the organization's jurisdiction extends over an ever larger area of economic and political activity, America and the rest of the world will have to deal with it ever more frequently, and treat it with the respect appropriate to a great power. Fortunately, the U.S. is uniquely positioned to benefit from the EU's still-changing character. Building on our long-standing relationships with the member states and the supranational European institutions, and engaging the EU in ever closer dialogue and collaboration, the U.S. can over the next several years help shape the larger transatlantic relationship in ways that serve our national interests as well as the many goals we share with Europe.

Beyond Brussels:
Dealing with the Member States

Finding out who speaks for Europe can be frustrating not only for outsiders. Often the Europeans themselves don't know who speaks for them.

The most spectacular example of this reality, in my experience and in the history of U.S.-EU relations, was the intra-European controversy over the Second Gulf War. EU member state governments were divided between those who joined the U.S.-led coalition of the willing and those, led by France and Germany, who opposed the use of force against Saddam Hussein. The EU institutions in Brussels reflected this internal split.

In an official statement on March 21, 2003, the day after the start of Operation Iraqi Freedom, Romano Prodi, then-President of the Commission, expressed dismay at the "onslaught of war," and regretted the lack of a common European stand, but he did not condemn the invasion as such. (The following year, however, President Prodi praised Spain's withdrawal from the U.S.-led coalition and called for his own nation, Italy, to follow suit.)

Less than the two months before the invasion, the European Parliament (whose structure and functions, along with those of the other EU institutions, are outlined in appendix A) passed a resolution rejecting the use of force "without an explicit decision of the United Nations Security Council"; yet after the war began, members of Parliament (MEPs) critical of the U.S. could not summon the votes for a condemnation.

Javier Solana, High Representative for the Common Foreign and Security Policy, and thus the closest thing to an EU foreign minister at the time, took care not to antagonize either side of the dispute. At a meeting in February 2003 with Nick Burns, then our ambassador to

NATO, and myself, Solana stressed his hope that we could insulate U.S.-EU relations from any fallout over Iraq. This brought home to me the strange truth that, on the greatest source of transatlantic discord in recent years, the EU itself took no position.

It is tempting to conclude from this episode that American leaders and diplomats should simply bypass EU institutions and deal only with the member states. After all, our bilateral relationships with European nations go back far (in some cases, such as France, all the way to the American Revolution), and it is the member states that ultimately determine policy and law for the EU as a whole. National governments appoint the College of Commissioners, members of the European Parliament are elected on national slates, and no EU legislation can become law without approval of the member-state governments. It may therefore seem easier and more effective to pick up the phone and dial Paris, Berlin, or London, or all twenty-five capitals if necessary, than to wander into Brussels's bureaucratic maze.

This attitude is still common in Washington, where the twenty-five State Department officers responsible for the EU member states, each of whom concentrates on bilateral relations between that country and the U.S., are grouped into regional "desks": Western Europe, Nouthern Europe, the Baltic states, and so on. A separate desk handles EU affairs, along with those relating to the Organization for Economic Co-operation and Development (OECD) and the G8 group of major industrial democracies (two international organizations which, unlike the EU, include the U.S. as a member). Thus we handle our bilateral relationships with the EU member states largely without regard to the multilateral organization that increasingly determines those very countries' laws and policies.

One-on-one dealing with European nations is doomed to be increasingly ineffective, as the EU member states grow ever less free to act autonomously, even in areas where they remain in theory entirely sovereign, such as military defense. During our negotiations over the EU's Galileo satellite navigation system (which I discussed in chapter 4), every time we approached the governments of individual nations to voice our security concerns, they made clear that they could not help us. As far as they were concerned, satellite navigation was not fundamentally a matter of security but of transportation; and since the

Commission is responsible for transportation policy, they had handed over negotiating authority to Brussels. On the same grounds—that Galileo was not a defense project—European governments (in particular the French) blocked our attempts to raise the issue in NATO, our preferred multilateral forum for transatlantic security issues.

Something similar occurred in the law enforcement realm with the Container Security Initiative. The U.S. had already started to negotiate with several individual member states for an arrangement that would allow us to search cargo containers on U.S.-bound ships before they left European ports, an important part of our antiterrorism strategy. Along came the EU's Transportation Commissioner Loyola De Palacio, who told me that we had to negotiate with her instead. Fortunately, the agreements we had been working out separately with the national governments were eventually subsumed in a single agreement with the EU in 2003.

Results have been less satisfactory in our dealings over the International Criminal Court (ICC). With American military personnel and civilians around the world potential targets of politicized prosecutions and investigations, the U.S. has sought bilateral agreements (called "Article 98s," after the relevant portion of the treaty that created the ICC), which prohibit the surrender of U.S. citizens or employees to the ICC without our government's consent. Over 90 sovereign countries have signed these "nonsurrender" agreements to date, but EU member states have refused to negotiate with us. They say that they are bound by a common EU policy which limits the scope of any such agreements to U.S. military, diplomatic, and consular personnel. Several aspiring member states have also refused to negotiate with us on this matter lest they harm their chances of joining the EU. As European integration continues, frustrations of this kind in our bilateral dealings with European governments are going to become only more common.

This does not mean that European nation-states no longer matter, or that the U.S. can afford to turn all its diplomatic attention to Brussels. Even as member states grow less powerful in what they can do on their own, they grow more powerful through their ability to influence the EU as whole. Much EU law and policy, even though it officially starts as a proposal by the Commission, actually originates in the national capitals. Nor can any legislation pass without the consent of the member states; and even after it becomes law, national governments take a big hand in determining how it is implemented.

Sometimes even a single government can hold up action by all the rest. France was able to force the EU to let lapse a travel ban on Zimbabwean officials briefly in early 2003, so that the dictator Robert Mugabe could attend a France-Africa summit in Paris. Cyprus, the third-smallest member in terms of population, has been able to decide whether the other twenty-four member states may offer trade privileges to Turkish-occupied northern Cyprus, as part of a solution to the island's three-decade-long division. The Republic of Cyprus could in theory stop the EU from accepting Turkey into its ranks.

In most cases, one or two states will not veto a policy supported by all the rest. As in any political grouping, members have a long-term incentive to compromise. Sweden has gone along with efforts to lift the arms embargo on China, and the Czech Republic has accepted easing diplomatic sanctions on Castro's Cuba, despite misgivings in both cases over human rights abuses by the non-European countries. Luxembourg has given in to EU pressure and agreed to withhold tax on bank accounts held by nonresidents, undermining its lucrative status as a tax haven. Britain swallowed its objections to restrictions on economic freedom in the Charter of Fundamental Rights and allowed that document to be included (with some limits on its application) in the 2004 constitutional treaty.

Member-state power extends beyond intergovernmental matters—that is, policy areas in which each country holds a veto—into what is formally the supranational domain, where authority is supposed to rest entirely with Brussels. Members of the European Commission swear to act "in the general interest of the Community" and "neither seek nor take instructions from any government" during their term of office.[1] But of course commissioners do not break ties to their home countries, and these ties can influence their actions on the most contentious matters. It was no coincidence in 2003 that the two German members of the Commission, Michaela Schreyer and Günter Verheugen, pushed to water down a directive that would have facilitated foreign takeovers of European corporations, since that legislation would have interfered with Berlin's policy of maintaining Volkswagen and other large companies as "national champions."

All this means that America's traditional bilateral relations with the EU's twenty-five national governments remain vitally important—but that they increasingly matter less for their own sake than as facets of our relationship with the EU as a whole. Our embassies in the member-state capitals, when they deal with national governments or report back to Washington on the situation in their host countries, must therefore take ever greater account of the EU dimension to every issue.

My work in Brussels would not have been possible without the insights and collaboration of my American colleagues "on the ground" in every EU country. Across the gamut of policy areas, from environmental regulation to military defense, our embassy's ability to influence the EU institutions depended on close cooperation with American embassies in every EU member state. Accordingly, our mission in Brussels tried whenever possible to inform and coordinate the EU-related activities of U.S. diplomatic personnel across the continent—for instance, by bringing nationally based officers to Brussels for conferences on various fields, including law enforcement, public diplomacy, and economic affairs.

Our most ambitious effort of this kind was the chiefs of mission conference in March 2002. This event brought the American envoys to all EU member states to Brussels, where they met with top officials of the EU and NATO and heard presentations on the pan-European ramifications of their bilateral diplomatic work. Many of the ambassadors told me afterwards that they returned to their host countries with a greater appreciation of the policy-making links between member-state capitals and the EU institutions.

Russia and Japan, which understand the need for a coordinated approach to Europe, both hold such meetings of their EU-based diplomats on a regular basis; and I believe we should do likewise, at least once a year.

The chiefs of mission conference also led to a formal State Department review of our European policy, officially presented to then–National Security Advisor Condoleeza Rice in January 2003, which in turn led to enhanced personnel training and interagency coordination on EU matters and a more assertive effort to publicize the U.S. point of view on transatlantic issues.

There is much more we could do to coordinate our bilateral relationships with European nations and our relationship with the EU. All of our ambassadors to EU member states and would-be member states should be briefed on the management of EU relations before they start their jobs; and each of our missions in Europe should have at least one foreign service officer dedicated to EU affairs. As the center for coordinating our representation in Europe, our mission in Brussels should be upgraded, with the appointment of two deputy ambassadors to handle economic and political-security issues (on the model of the EU member states' own delegations to Brussels). This would leave our senior ambassador free to concentrate on high-level representation and travel to national capitals, the latter an increasingly important part of the job, since he or she represents the U.S. not just to the EU but to all the member states as well. Back in Washington, the State Department should end its balkanized approach to Europe and gather all the officers responsible for EU member states and aspirant countries into a single bureau of EU affairs. This bureau should be headed by an assistant secretary, with the support of four deputy assistant secretaries specializing in security, political, economic, and global affairs. I realize that this proposal will strike some in Washington as radical, but the growth and character of the EU dictates that we make changes along these lines, and the sooner the better.

Coordinating our bilateral and EU relationships is vital to the success of our diplomacy, because every EU member state is a potential source of information about what happens in Brussels and a potential advocate for our positions within the EU institutions. Influencing the EU, therefore, entails courting and collaborating with national governments. This has nothing to do with any supposed strategy of "divide and conquer." It is the logical consequence of how the EU has chosen to run itself: through member-state coalitions that shift according to each government's pursuit of its national interest.

Critics should no more expect America to stop talking with European governments about EU affairs than they should expect foreign countries to stop lobbying the U.S. Congress.

EU member states are helpful to America insofar as their interests and views match up with our own; and these alignments vary according to the law or policy in question. No EU government will agree or disagree with the U.S. on every issue, so we must constantly search for areas of common interest with them all. For example, notwithstanding our many differences with France, President Jacques Chirac has proved a key ally to the U.S. in efforts to make the Commission's proposed regime for chemicals testing more business-friendly. The French President's support for Turkey's accession to the EU, contrary to majority opinion in his own country, also coincides with U.S. policy. Similarly, Germany, despite its deep disagreements with the U.S. over Iraq, has strongly backed our efforts to broker increased cooperation in Europe against terrorism, most prominently in supporting new agreements on extradition and the sharing of data with U.S. intelligence and law enforcement agencies.

By the same token, it would be shortsighted to take for granted even our most reliable collaborators, such as Britain or the post-Communist Central and Eastern countries, whose pro-Americanism was so conspicuous before and during the Second Gulf War. Not only do governments change at the will of the electorate (as happened in Spain, our former Iraq ally, in March 2004), but a nation's sentiments toward the U.S. can sour when insufficiently cultivated. Poland backed the U.S. in its policy toward Saddam Hussein and contributed the fourth-largest contingent of troops to the coalition in Iraq; yet none of the lucrative contracts for Iraq's reconstruction went to Polish companies until more than a year after the invasion. As of this writing, Polish citizens were still not able to enter the U.S. without a visa, a privilege enjoyed by twenty-seven nations including France. In February 2005, at a Brussels meeting of Secretary of State Condoleeza Rice and her EU counterparts, I heard the foreign ministers of Poland and several other Central and Eastern European states complain forcefully about the visa issue. As these countries begin to experience the benefits of EU membership, in the forms of agricultural subsidies and larger markets, public opinion surveys and statements by political and business leaders convey growing frustration with America, a feeling for which we could end up paying the price in Brussels.

Dealing with the EU Institutions

Compared with our ties with individual European countries, America's relationship with the EU itself is of recent vintage. Yet we have been there from the start, since the distinguished diplomat David Bruce presented his credentials as the first U.S. representative to the European Coal and Steel Community in 1953. Thanks to America's historic role as sponsor and defender of European integration, our representatives have long enjoyed a privileged place among non-European envoys to the EU.

In November 2003, fifty years after Ambassador Bruce's arrival, then–Secretary of State Colin Powell met in Brussels with his counterparts from the twenty-five EU member states, the first time that a U.S. secretary of state had met with the EU foreign ministers sitting all together as the General and External Relations Council. As the U.S. envoy at that time, I took satisfaction in helping to bring that event about, along with my Italian colleague, Ambassador Umberto Vattani, because I considered it one of my key missions to help our senior leadership, as well as the American public, appreciate the growing importance of European integration. My hopes and efforts of three and a half years found a satisfying conclusion in the visits of President Bush and Secretary of State Rice in February 2005, when both of them publicly recognized and declared their support for a strong and unified Europe.

In this period of dramatic change within the EU, and of continuing tension in the transatlantic relationship, it is vital that America continue to talk and work as much as possible with the supranational EU institutions, on areas of agreement and disagreement alike. By extending our dialogue through all possible avenues, and by intensifying our collaboration in every area of common interest, the U.S. can help to ensure a stronger partnership with an ever stronger EU. The closer we engage the EU at every level, the more likely it is that we will know whom to call—and what to say—when the need arises.

Our most prominent opportunity for dialogue is the annual U.S.-EU summit, where the American president joins the head of state or government of the country currently holding the EU presidency, along with the President of the European Commission, the Commissioner for External Relations, and the EU's High Representative for the Common Foreign and Security Policy, to discuss the most pressing issues in transatlantic relations. Other influential parties are also sometimes included. At one of the summits I attended, in Dromoland Castle, Ireland, in June 2004, business leaders from the U.S. and the EU, representing the newly reconstituted Transatlantic Business Dialogue (TABD), presented their recommendations for strengthening commercial relations between the world's two largest economies.

Presidential summits began in 1990, when the EU was still known as the European Community, and today they represent the highest level of dialogue in a diplomatic framework called the New Transatlantic Agenda (NTA), established in 1995 following a proposal by my predecessor, Ambassador Stuart E. Eizenstat. The NTA has been the basis for regular meetings between U.S. officials and their EU counterparts (four times a year at the level of undersecretary, and monthly at the level of assistant or deputy assistant secretary) as well as unofficial transatlantic dialogues involving the business community and nongovernmental organizations.

Because the EU's organizational structure is so complex, an American official typically meets not with one, but with a so-called "troika" of EU counterparts: one from the Commission, one from the government of the particular member state that currently holds the rotating EU presidency, and one from the member state next in line for the presidency. (A representative of the Council secretariat, which represents the member states collectively, usually attends these meetings as an observer.) The troika format is also used when specialists on the staff of our mission in Brussels meet with EU officials at their level. Some troikas are organized around regional themes, such as Africa, Latin America, East Asia, South Asia, the western Balkans, and so on. Others deal with global issues such as counterterrorism, disarmament, nonproliferation, and the United Nations.

These meetings are an indispensable way to learn what the various EU players think about particular issues, what legislation or initiatives might be in the pipeline, and who the driving forces are behind certain EU policies. But unless the EU has clearly articulated a common policy on an issue, we also need to speak to the ambassadors of the twenty-five member states in Brussels. It takes a long time for a diplomat in Brussels to discover who the key people are on any given issue. It usually turns out that there are two or three, working in any combination of the Commission, Council, or member-state ministries. The appointment of a single EU foreign minister would simplify our relations with regard to those foreign policy questions on which there exists a common EU position. But many of the most ticklish transatlantic issues will be those on which member states cannot agree. For the foreseeable future, as the EU grows more ambitious in the reach of its policies, there will be only more people for us to talk with.

A conspicuous absence from the troika format is any representative of the EU's legislative branch. Strictly speaking, the European Parliament has no authority over foreign policy. Yet in my visits to Strasbourg, France, where Parliament holds its plenary sessions, and in the meetings I organized between parliamentary leaders and senior American officials, including President Bush, I noticed a growing assertiveness by the European legislature—with regard not only to EU legislation but also to relations with the United States. As Pat Cox, who was president of Parliament until 2004, often stressed to me, this increasingly powerful body does decide a range of matters with great impact on international affairs and on transatlantic relations in particular.

For instance, Parliament must approve all EU grants of development assistance, such as the Commission's $200 million in annual support for the reconstruction of Iraq. Any EU program of economic incentives for Iran to cease developing nuclear weapons would also require parliamentary approval. During my tenure, Parliament's consent was necessary before the U.S. and the EU could reach agreement on the sensitive security question of sharing personal data on airline passengers.

Although members of Parliament (MEPs) cannot actually initiate legislation, they can amend it in significant ways, as when they required food products with no trace of genetically modified organisms (GMOs) to be labeled "genetically modified," so long as any such organisms had been used in the production process. As a result, ordinary potato chips are considered "genetically modified" if they have been fried in GMO soybean oil. Since such a label renders a product practically impossible to sell in Europe, Parliament took care to exempt certain products made in the EU from the stricter standard.

Parliament also has the power to reject nominees for the European Commission. In a sign of its increasing self-confidence, in 2004 it forced two such nominees to withdraw and another to be assigned a different portfolio than what President Barroso had originally chosen.

Much of Parliament's influence is not direct, in the form of legislation or exercise of constitutional prerogatives, but derives from its prominence as a pan-European soapbox. Through resolutions and committee hearings calculated to grab the attention of the 1,000-plus accredited EU journalists in Brussels, MEPs can make their voices heard across the continent. While these voices fall along the widest political spectrum imaginable, the loudest are all too often unsympathetic or downright hostile to America. The ultimate reason for this, in my view, is the relatively low sense of responsibility still prevailing in a body with no direct role in governance and no direct stake in transatlantic harmony. Members eager for publicity—and attacking the sole superpower is a sure way of getting it—feel free to say what they like. Therefore, when President Bush visited the EU institutions in February 2005, one of the reasons that we did not seek to have him address Parliament was a concern, shared by parliamentary leaders themselves, that some MEPs would disrupt the speech with a protest. But as the legislature's responsibilities increase, the likelihood of such displays should diminish.

Although Parliament is still a much less important body within its own system than is the U.S. Congress, dialogue between the two can help avoid the legal conflicts that are a growing hazard in our increasingly interdependent systems. "There is the risk of extraterritorial spill-over effects when legislating at the continental level," notes former President Cox, pointing to data privacy, financial and accounting standards, and environmental regulation as areas in which lawmakers can benefit from an "early warning system" to help avoid unnecessary conflicts.

More generally, as Cox tells me, both sides would benefit from a greater awareness of how they think and do business. As he puts it, "Americans see Europeans as men from Mars who don't even speak English. Europeans think Americans are cowboys obsessed with security. That's a prescription for trouble. Dialogue avoids stereotype. Then you can see where a problem is shared, and look at differences in approach."

Congress and Parliament already exchange delegations twice a year, and I think we should make this dialogue more frequent, extending it to the committee level to make it more substantive. As lawmakers and elected politicians, the members of both bodies are natural interlocutors. Getting them together more often could reduce the quantity and virulence of anti-American rhetoric in Parliament, and raise awareness of Europe in Congress. A recent sign that Capitol Hill is growing more interested in Europe was the formation in May 2005 of the House EU Caucus, a bipartisan group of lawmakers seeking a greater understanding of the EU and its relations with the United States.

A crucial though unofficial channel for legislative dialogue is the Transatlantic Policy Network (TPN), which brings together MEPs and U.S. senators and congressmen, as well as European and American business leaders and academics, who seek ways to strengthen U.S.-EU cooperation. TPN was a formative influence on the New Transatlantic Agenda framework in 1995, and its notable recent efforts include a campaign to establish a Barrier-Free Transatlantic Marketplace by 2015. Parliament has endorsed this and other TPN goals in resolutions whose language is virtually identical to that of the network's recommendations, demonstrating the power of an organization able to develop ideas and feed them into the political system.

Such mechanisms for transatlantic consultation are invaluable, yet there is no substitute for strong personal relationships between the principals on both sides. An outstanding and unlikely example of such a relationship in my experience is that between Pascal Lamy and Robert Zoellick, who served as the top EU and U.S. trade negotiators during my tenure in Brussels. Despite their differences in culture and ideology, Lamy and Zoellick—respectively, a French Socialist with pronounced dirigiste tendencies, and a conservative, free-market Republican—developed the highest levels of trust and respect for each other in nearly four years of working together. Because the two men keenly appreciated the value of the enormous transatlantic commercial relationship, they were ever careful to prevent disputes over particular trade issues from affecting their negotiations over others. They always kept the big picture in mind.

Even when unable to resolve differences on their own, Zoellick and Lamy moderated their responses to avoid friction that might have led to trade wars. For instance, after the World Trade Organization (WTO) ruled that the EU could impose up to $4 billion in annual tariffs on U.S. goods, as punishment for federal tax breaks on American companies' foreign earnings, the Commission chose on Lamy's recommendation not to impose the tariffs all at once but to phase them in slowly, giving Congress time to change the law. Coming after an especially acrimonious period in transatlantic trade negotiations during the late 1990s, the Zoellick-Lamy era was one of remarkable harmony. It was therefore a happy day for U.S.-EU relations when Bob Zoellick joined the State Department as Secretary Rice's deputy in early 2005 (along with another experienced Brussels hand, Nick Burns, former ambassador to NATO, in the department's number-three job of under secretary for political affairs); and a no less propitious occasion when Lamy was named director-general of the WTO later the same year. We should build on the Zoellick-Lamy model by encouraging more face-to-face dealings between U.S. officials and their Commission counterparts. A strong transatlantic relationship depends on strong personal relationships at the highest levels.

Although the U.S. and the EU continue to disagree over significant trade issues—notably, over public assistance to the aerospace firms Boeing and Airbus—the biggest future threats to the flow of transatlantic commerce are likely to come not in the traditional forms of tariffs and nontariff barriers but in conflicting regulations and product standards. As noted in chapter 3, divergences in European and American regulatory regimes stem from historically rooted differences in economic philosophy. Although these differences will not be easy to resolve, the more that regulators from both sides talk to each other, the better able they will be to minimize conflicts, or at least anticipate them, and thus mitigate their impact on industry. American and European regulators already meet each other periodically through the Financial Markets Dialogue and the Consumer Protection Dialogue, which could serve as models for forums in other areas, including environmental protection. Exchange programs, with EU and U.S. regulators working on each other's turf, would deepen awareness of the most consequential differences in our regulatory cultures.

While total harmonization in official product standards grows ever less likely, as the EU continues to impose specifications that the U.S. deems excessively stringent, proposals for *voluntary* harmonization by private industry groups on both sides of the Atlantic do hold promise. More generally, communication at the private-sector level can go far to defuse or circumvent regulatory conflicts. When, in September 2003, the governments of Germany, France, and Britain called on the Commission President to modify the proposed chemicals testing regime, REACH, in ways that would make it more hospitable to American products, they were responding to pressure from the European chemicals industry, which was acting in a coordinated effort with its U.S. competitors to achieve their common goal of a more business-friendly regulatory regime.

The revival in 2004 of the Transatlantic Business Dialogue, made up of European and American corporate leaders as well as top policy makers from both sides, was a major boost for communication and collaboration. There is plenty of scope for more specialized forums, too. During my tenure in Brussels, our mission facilitated meetings of American and European executives in the financial services industry, a field of especially urgent concern today as the EU moves toward a single market for money and stocks and both Europe and America tighten their supervision of banks, brokers, and accountants. Investors and entrepreneurs in both the U.S. and the EU have an enormous amount to lose or gain, depending on how compatible we can make our financial rules. Nor is such dialogue limited to business. The Transatlantic Consumers Dialogue (TACD), which brings together over sixty U.S. and EU consumer groups, is one of several transatlantic forums for other stakeholders including organized labor and public interest groups.

Communication between European and American stakeholders does more than help resolve problems affecting a particular industry. As it strengthens the transatlantic commercial relationship, such dialogue brings the relationship's importance to the attention of political leaders and thus helps stabilize U.S.-EU relations. For example, pressure from the TABD has improved the odds of reducing telecom tariffs in the context of the WTO's "Doha Round" of negotiations. The TABD has also helped accelerate the process of regulatory reform on both sides of the ocean, including in the area of financial services. And amid the transatlantic political friction during the run-up to the Second Gulf War, the determination of EU and U.S. corporate leaders to keep doing business as usual meant that trade and investment flows in this period actually *increased*. That helps explain why disagreements over Iraq did not spill over into other areas of the transatlantic relationship.

The most prominent structures for transatlantic consultation and dialogue are the international organizations in which Europe and the United States are both represented. These include broad-agenda institutions such as the Organization for Economic Co-operation and Development (OECD), successor to the entity that administered the Marshall Plan; and the Organization for Security and Co-operation in Europe (OSCE), which is active in conflict prevention, crisis management, and postconflict rehabilitation. We also deal with Europe in more specialized forums such as the International Civil Aviation Organization (ICAO) and the Codex Alimentarius Commission, which is primarily concerned with food standards. Transatlantic trade negotiations take place within the framework of the WTO.

Dealing with Europe in the context of such forums can be effective because the EU, as the multilateral organization par excellence, is particularly susceptible to their soft power. Ambassador Richard Morningstar, my predecessor in Brussels, recalls that the Commission finally compromised over a contentious question of how to reduce aircraft engine noise (when proposed EU regulations would have left the U.S.-based manufacturer United Technologies at a gross disadvantage to European competitors) only after the solution was hammered out at ICAO: "The fact that there was a multilateral organization allowed us to say, 'if you don't come to some resolution with us within this international organization then you, ironically, will be acting unilaterally.'"

Multilateral solutions have a recognized legitimacy that makes them more durable: the more states that sign on to an agreement, the less basis any will have on which to second-guess it later on. Since the most pressing issues in transatlantic relations are actually global in scope, international forums are often the most fitting contexts for agreements between the U.S. and the EU.

Unfortunately, multilateral forums are also where the U.S. has the most difficulty in negotiating with Europe, because the representatives of EU member states typically come to international organizations with little flexibility to deal, having already hammered out an EU consensus position in Brussels. At worst, meetings can turn into a "zero-sum" competition between the U.S. and the EU to enlist other countries in support of our respective positions. Ideally, we should resolve differences with the EU in advance, then work together in the international forums to achieve our common goals.

A success story of this kind, on the heels of a well-publicized breakdown in transatlantic comity, occurred at the United Nations Commission on Human Rights (UNCHR). In 2001, EU member states helped vote the U.S. off of the Commission for the first time since its establishment over half a century earlier—not for the ideological reasons reported in the press (to protest the Bush administration's stand on the ICC and the Kyoto Protocol on global warming), but simply to make room for more EU members on the fifty-three-seat body. The U.S. regained its seat the following year, but more significantly, for six months beginning in the late summer of 2002, we worked closely with the EU to prepare for the 2003 session. Lorne W. Craner, the U.S. Assistant Secretary of State for Democracy, Human Rights and Labor, and members of our Brussels mission staff met and talked frequently with EU representatives in that period to put together a common program. As a result, the Commission's fifty-ninth session, held March 17–April 25, 2003, was acknowledged by the head of our delegation, Ambassador Jeanne Kirkpatrick, as one of the most successful ever, with a high degree of transatlantic agreement on topics including assistance for refugees, prevention and treatment of HIV/AIDS, and measures against religious intolerance. Most remarkable is that none of the transatlantic discord over the Second Gulf War impeded our collaboration at the UNCHR, even though the session started just three days after the invasion of Iraq.

Working Together

For all the value of dialogue (and I wouldn't be a diplomat if I didn't believe in it), there is no substitute for working together as a means of building trust, sharing best practices, learning how a partner thinks and operates, and setting the basis for further collaboration. America already works with the EU on a wide range of areas; and as European integration brings more and more authority to Brussels, the EU potentially becomes an ever more effective partner. By intensifying and extending our cooperation in areas of common interest, the U.S. can get to know the EU better and establish the foundations for a relationship of lasting harmony and productivity.

One of the great untold success stories of transatlantic relations has been the joint U.S.-EU record of assistance to poor countries, not only in response to humanitarian crises such as earthquakes, civil wars, and the South Asian tsunami of December 2004 but for longer-term economic development all over the world. Coordination is vital to ensuring that the money we spend—$59 billion in development assistance in 2003, a quarter of it contributed by the U.S.—goes where it is needed. The U.S. and the EU share expertise, and by working together we reduce the opportunities for waste and corruption that come with redundant giving. If Americans donate $100 million to help a country train its judiciary, for example, it makes no sense for the EU to donate the equivalent in euros for the same purpose.

Apart from the humanitarian motive, assistance often ties in with geopolitical aims, and here too we have worked well with Europe. At the Madrid donors conference in 2003, EU nations pledged $1.4 billion for the reconstruction of Iraq. Since the invasion, the Commission has distributed $200 million a year in Iraq and was especially helpful in the run-up to elections there in January 2005.

Although the EU brings more public money to the table, it is less flexible than the U.S. in disbursing it. The Commission sets a five-year budget for development assistance, whereas the U.S. makes a budget every year, allowing us to respond more swiftly to unanticipated needs, such as the reconstruction of Afghanistan or Iraq. The U.S. has far more experience than Europe of making alliances with private-sector donors, which together give up to four times as much as the U.S. government.

The U.S. has been also been much more inclined than the EU to link development assistance to political and economic reform in the recipient nations, a philosophy of giving exemplified by the Millennium Challenge Account, which President Bush has described as "devoted to projects in nations that govern justly, invest in their people and encourage economic freedom." Although the EU's European Neighborhood Policy, of assistance to countries in North Africa, the Middle East, and the former Soviet Union, formally encourages a commitment to "the rule of law, good governance, the respect for human rights, including minority rights, the promotion of good neighbor relations, and the principles of market economy and sustainable development," the EU does not make its donations contingent on the recipients' records in any of these areas.

A largely unheralded field of transatlantic cooperation, where America's interests and policies have been almost perfectly congruent with those of Europe, is the former Soviet Union. Both the U.S. and the EU have a clear interest in seeing Russia and its neighbors become stable, democratic countries with free economies. Accordingly, State Department officials and their counterparts at the EU institutions and member-state foreign ministries keep each other well briefed on all relevant issues, as do U.S. and European diplomatic missions throughout the former USSR. In all of this collaboration, our embassy in Brussels is often a crucial facilitator and intermediary. Washington and Brussels have coordinated their public diplomatic acts for maximum impact—for instance, by imposing simultaneous U.S. and EU visa bans on senior Belarus government officials in 2002–2003, and again in 2004, to protest the authoritarian policies of President Alexander Lukashenko.

We also work together in less obvious ways. Ukraine's "Orange Revolution" in late 2004 was rightly seen as a tribute to Europe's soft power, since membership in the EU was one of Viktor Yushchenko's rallying cries in his ultimately successful struggle for the presidency. The primary mediators in the Ukrainian crisis were Javier Solana of the European Council, and the presidents of two EU member states: Poland's Aleksander Kwasniewski and Lithuania's Valdas Adamkus. But U.S. support was also essential, in the form of aid and encouragement to pro-democracy forces before the election and in Secretary Powell's clear message to both Kiev and Moscow that the Ukrainian people should be free to choose their own leaders.

Unfortunately, not all EU leaders have been equally enthusiastic about Ukraine's turn to the West. At the NATO summit in Brussels in February 2005, where President Bush told President Yushchenko that the "door [was] open" to Ukrainian membership, pending the necessary political and economic reforms in his country, the leaders of France and Germany were conspicuous by their silence on the subject. Whereas British Prime Minister Tony Blair met with Yushchenko in Brussels, French President Chirac pointedly left a meeting shortly after the Ukrainian leader's arrival. France and Germany are evidently reluctant to embrace the former Soviet republic for fear of displeasing Russia. Remembering the Paris-Berlin-Moscow axis that opposed U.S. policy toward Saddam Hussein, I can only say that it would be a tremendous loss if our common U.S.-EU policy toward the former USSR—with all its potential benefits for the security, freedom, and prosperity of that troubled region—should fall prey to a Euro-Gaullist strategy of "multipolarity."

Instead, both the U.S. and the EU should be searching for additional areas of common interest. As the EU develops its common foreign and security policy, and insofar as that policy is compatible with our own, the U.S. should attempt to cooperate with it as much as possible: encouraging contacts between policy makers and diplomats at all levels, synchronizing our demarches, and so forth. By reducing the opportunities for other countries to pit Europe and America against each other, such coordination would allow us both to pursue our own policies more effectively.

No less important, the experience of working together builds trust on both sides, at the highest policy-making levels. The more we coordinate with the EU, the more comfortable Washington becomes about sharing information with Brussels and vice versa, opening up possibilities for further cooperation. No policy maker who has dealt with the other side on issues where U.S. and EU policies coincide is apt to define our relationship based merely on our differences. So when the inevitable disagreements come, the experience of cooperation helps moderate disappointment and encourage the search for compromise.

With heightened efforts to combat international terrorism since 9/11, law enforcement has been a growing area of transatlantic collaboration; and as the EU member states transfer more authority in this realm to the EU itself, more of this collaboration will be between Washington and Brussels. In 2003, I signed treaties between the EU and the U.S. on extradition and mutual legal assistance, which I hope the U.S. Senate will ratify by 2007. In the past, the U.S. would have made such agreements with the individual member states, not with the EU itself. This in itself made the event historic, but it matters for other reasons as well. Under the mutual legal assistance treaty, American authorities would be able to locate a bank account under a given name anywhere in the EU, and European officials would be able to do likewise in the United States. This would facilitate the identification of illicit accounts, whether used for organized crime, drug trafficking, or terrorism. Just as significant, the treaty would permit the formation of joint American-European strike forces, made up of both investigators and prosecutors working alongside each other from the start of an inquiry right up through the prosecution. By way of example, this could mean integrating FBI agents into a multinational team under local leadership in Germany in order to investigate an international conspiracy like the one that produced the 9/11 attacks.

Apart from enhancing our ability to pursue specific cases, such strike forces will turn out American law enforcement personnel with a deeper understanding of the EU. We should promote such understanding in all federal employees who deal with Europe. At the moment, only the State Department offers any instruction in how the EU works or why it matters. A two-week EU course offered by the

Department's Foreign Service Institute in Arlington, Virginia, is open to military and civilian personnel from other departments who are assigned to European posts. But as the Department's review of EU policy concluded in 2002, many officials who rarely leave Washington, such as regulators, also need to learn the nuts and bolts of Brussels.[2]

No area of transatlantic collaboration is more sensitive or consequential than military defense. For more than half a century, the security relationship between the U.S. and Europe has been embodied in the North Atlantic Treaty Organization, a group of sovereign nation-states of which America is the undisputed leader. NATO remains the greatest peacetime military coalition ever assembled, and though its original raison d'être of defense against the Soviet Union has disappeared, its peacekeeping work in Afghanistan and elsewhere demonstrates its continuing value as a force for global stability.

The U.S. is more determined and able than ever to fulfill its commitments to European security. Although we have cut back our troop deployments in Europe since the end of the Cold War, and will continue to do so, technology now lets us move faster and farther than ever. The U.S. Air Force can engage in combat anywhere in the world within twenty-four hours; and bringing our troops back to the States actually enhances their effectiveness, by shortening the logistics chain, producing economies of scale, and saving resources that would otherwise be spent on unnecessary installations abroad. Closing U.S. bases in Germany, or anywhere else, does not indicate any weakening of the Atlantic alliance.

What has changed, as I came to see during my tenure in Brussels, is that Europeans are beginning to develop a common military identity that does not include the United States. As I explained in chapter 4, the EU is no longer just an economic organization; it is an entity increasingly able and willing to project geopolitical power on its own. Although I believe that Europe's interests are fundamentally congruent with America's, we are bound to have differences of vision and strategy, especially now that the U.S. has ceased to play our Cold War leadership role. In order to reduce the potential for conflicts that could interfere with our collaboration along so many fronts—from humanitarian assistance to the promotion of free trade—it is urgent that the U.S. establish and cultivate a security relationship with the EU.

Many in Washington fiercely resist the idea of engaging the Europeans on security matters in any multilateral forum other than NATO. Traditionalists insist that recognizing the EU as a security organization would weaken NATO and hence the Atlantic alliance. They reason that since NATO includes nineteen out of the EU's twenty-five member states, and all the EU members with significant military capability, we should be able to address any transatlantic security issues in that forum.

Unfortunately, not all Europeans think likewise. German Chancellor Gerhard Schröder was certainly exaggerating when he declared in February 2005 that NATO was "no longer the primary venue where transatlantic partners discuss and coordinate strategies." And when French President Chirac endorsed Schröder's statement shortly thereafter, it was easy to infer the influence of Euro-Gaullism. Yet whatever those leaders' motivations may have been, it is clear that NATO no longer offers us the opportunity to address all our security concerns involving Europe.

The officials who represent European states in NATO are not the same officials who represent those states in the EU, and these separate groups tend not to share information with each other. While the U.S. has a permanent representative on the North Atlantic Council, which runs NATO, we are not represented on the EU's Political and Security Committee or the General and External Affairs Council; and that makes it increasingly hard to get our questions answered or our concerns heard on many security issues.

The EU's emergence as a security organization is a logical, and virtually inevitable, consequence of European integration. Whether or not we choose to dignify it with our recognition, the EU's security and defense policy is going to move forward. Engaging with that reality is the best way to keep the EU from competing or conflicting with our interests, whether under the influence of Euro-Gaullism or merely from a lack of foresight. Establishing a security relationship with the EU, to complement our bilateral relationships with the individual EU member states and our multilateral relationship with Europe through NATO, would do nothing to weaken the Atlantic alliance. On the contrary, *failing* to establish such a relationship is the surest way to remain oblivious to potential conflicts until it is too late to avoid them.

To put it in positive terms, a formal security relationship with the EU is indispensable to a comprehensive strategic partnership with Europe, in areas including military cooperation and extending to humanitarian and development assistance, promotion of democracy, law enforcement, and intelligence. Such a partnership will be key to realizing our goals in the Middle East, the former USSR, and much of the world.

Dealing with the EU on security, as in most other areas, is a special challenge, not only because the EU has a multiplicity of power centers which are often in competition with each other, but because the structure of the organization is still changing, and bound to continue changing for the foreseeable future.

So, returning to Dr. Kissinger's question, whom do we call when we want to reach Europe? As I hope I have conveyed in this chapter, the answer is a complicated one, but the short version is: "It depends." There is not yet a single phone number, but at least there is a switchboard. Depending on the issue, authority (or as they say in Brussels, "competence") may lie with the Commission, the Council, or the governments of the individual member states; or it may be shared between two of these, or among all three. Parliament may also have an influence on the outcome, so that body too will need to be consulted and persuaded. In our dealings with the EU, America will have to show enormous patience and flexibility, as well as humility and respect, if we hope to see this new global power emerge as a new and great ally of the United States.

Notes

1. Treaty establishing the European Community, Article 213 (2). http://europa.eu.int/eur-lex/lex/en/treaties/index.htm.

2. As a gesture that I hope will encourage an interagency focus on Europe, I have endowed an annual award to "recognize outstanding efforts in advancing U.S. policy objectives through cooperation with the EU." All foreign service and civil service employees of the Departments of State, Commerce, and Agriculture and the U.S. Agency for International Development (USAID) are eligible. The first recipient, in 2004, was Ambassador Charles P. Ries, our envoy to Greece.

CHAPTER SEVEN

Lobbying the European Union

A few months after the European Commission blocked the merger of General Electric and Honeywell International, GE's CEO Jeff Immelt told me: "Here's the reason to be an active player in Europe." That same year, 2001, GE moved its European headquarters from London to Brussels and subsequently invested over $30 billion in EU companies.

GE is not alone. In the last twenty years, the American Chamber of Commerce to the European Union (AmCham EU) has seen membership more than triple. With well over half of the regulations that affect business in Europe originating in Brussels, and with non-European countries following the EU's lead in environmental and other standards, no company with global reach or aspirations can afford to overlook the EU factor.

In late 2004, over 5,000 accredited lobbyists were listed on the European Parliament's website. According to the chairman of Parliament's environment committee, there were actually about 20,000 lobbyists in Brussels, only 4,000 fewer than the total number of civil servants working for the Commission.[1] Neither of these figures includes the embassies of non-EU countries, such as the U.S. mission which I headed for over three and a half years, though of course these also help advance the interests of national industries (see below).

Lobbying has a long history in Europe. The word itself originally referred to a lobby in London's Palace of Westminster, where petitioners were permitted to approach members of parliament. But the modern practice has been perfected in the United States, and Europeans have borrowed many American techniques. U.S. companies themselves are naturally tempted, when dealing abroad, to use what's worked for them at home.

Like many exports, however, the American way of lobbying requires adjustments before it will sell in a foreign market. Despite the large degree of convergence between our economies recently, and the growing similarities between our business and political cultures, Brussels is still not Washington. And the differences in how these capitals work can be crucial to the interests of American corporations doing business on the other side of the Atlantic.

Everyone knows the caricatures: Gucci-loafered corporate touts lingering outside the U.S. Senate cloakroom, waiting to grab the ear of a committee chairman. Once-and-future administration officials ensconced in their K-Street offices, working their Rolodexes of the powerful on behalf of deep-pocketed clients. The grassroots impresario, a master of press relations and direct mail, pressuring legislators by mobilizing key segments of their constituencies for or against a certain bill.

Such images are, even with respect to Washington, oversimplifications of an increasingly sophisticated profession. When it comes to Brussels, the clichés are practically irrelevant.

In the capital of the EU, acquaintance with the powerful matters less than awareness of the legislative process. Arguments based on job creation and economic growth, so effective with American policy makers, must compete here with appeals to the less commercial values of the European social model.

Still, American businesses *can* make their voices heard in Brussels. Many U.S. companies have mastered the art of lobbying the EU, sometimes after costly misunderstandings. This chapter aims to make such misunderstandings rarer. Here I lay out some of the obstacles and opportunities that American companies face in their dealings with the EU, along with suggestions for making those dealings more productive. I draw throughout on the wisdom of the experts, the lobbyists themselves.

Who Are the Lobbyists?

The men and women representing business in Brussels fall into two broad categories: "in-house" employees of particular corporations, and independent consultants working for various clients at a time.

Corporations have for years been sending employees to represent them in Brussels, but lately they have been sending people of a different sort. Until recently, Brussels was seen in business circles as an end-of-career assignment, a low-stress last job before retirement. "They've been through sales, they've been through operations, they've been in marketing, they've moved around the company, so very senior people," says Susan Danger, managing director of AmCham EU, describing the traditional in-house lobbyists.

Such experience produces employees with deep knowledge of their company, but not of the EU and how it works. As the EU has grown bigger and more complex, businesses have learned that they need specialists to deal with it. Today a Brussels lobbyist, whether in-house or independent, is likelier to be in her thirties than her fifties; will typically hold a degree in European studies or a related field (perhaps from one of the major training grounds for EU officials, such as the College of Europe in Bruges, or the University of Leuven); and may have worked as an intern in the Commission or Parliament. As this profile suggests, European lobbying has matured as a profession.

That's one reason why U.S. companies, after years of sending Americans to represent them in Brussels, are more and more often hiring Europeans for the job. Today, reports Danger (who is British), Europeans regularly outnumber Americans at AmCham EU meetings. This offers many advantages, not the least of them linguistic. Even with English as the unofficial lingua franca of the EU, there's no substitute for a common mother tongue when it comes to persuading, or merely establishing rapport with, European officials. Hiring Europeans also helps U.S. businesses tap into the growing pool of experts in EU affairs.

Independent lobbyists in Brussels, whether they work for local public relations firms or for U.S.-based multinational consultancies, have similar backgrounds to their in-house colleagues and perform similar tasks—with one big difference. Whereas in-house employees often meet with EU officials on behalf of their companies, outside consultants almost never do. The latter remain behind the scenes, explaining the legislative process, suggesting when and with whom to speak, and helping to shape the way a client presents itself.

Outside consultants often take jobs as in-house lobbyists and vice versa, but the ultimate goal for many is a permanent job at the European Commission. Americans will find nothing odd in a career that mixes public service with private-sector employment. The difference is that, in the EU, the movement between private and public is overwhelmingly one-way. Brussels has no version of Washington's "revolving door." Few Commission officials, and hardly any commissioners themselves, ever leave to lobby their former institution.

One reason for this is that corporate lobbying is still less respectable in Europe than in the United States. The business world certainly holds allure for Europeans, and a number of ex-commissioners sit on corporate boards; but as long as lobbying is seen as a low-prestige activity, former EU officials will tend to shun it.

Another reason the Commission has no revolving door is that, once inside, nearly everyone prefers to stay. Commission officials enjoy an enviable standard of living. Their salaries are practically tax free and go far in Brussels, one of the most affordable European capitals. They get allowances for their children's education and for travel to their home countries, among many other benefits; and like most civil servants, they are virtually impossible to fire. Not for nothing is the Commission known in EU circles as the "Golden Cage."

Former members of the European Parliament (MEPs) are hardly more likely to become lobbyists. In their case, it's more a matter of low demand. Given Parliament's secondary role in the legislative process—limited to amending or rejecting proposals by the Commission—former MEPs rarely have much influence to sell. But *sitting* MEPs are another story. They are allowed to work for firms with interests before Parliament; and not surprisingly, a number of them do so. The German MEP Elmar Brok has for years combined his public duties with a job as Senior Vice President for Media Development at the media conglomerate Bertelsmann AG.

Getting In Early

The EU lawmaking process (outlined in appendix A) necessarily starts in the Commission, the only institution with the power to propose legislation. Before it can take force, a Commission proposal must be approved, either jointly by the Parliament and the Council, or by the Council alone.

The long and complicated gestation of EU law is a process that businesses must monitor closely from start to finish. Crucial provisions can creep in at the last minute and surprises can be costly. For instance, in 2003, two important directives on hazardous waste, originally applying only to consumer electronics, were extended in the last legislative phase to cover machinery.[2] Suddenly, an entire industry faced the prospect of obligations from which it had assumed it would be exempt. Taking common substances such as mercury out of a production process is enormously complicated and expensive even with plenty of advance notice. These companies had to do it in a few months.

While vigilance till the very end can save a company or industry from nasty shocks, the time window for influencing the process is much smaller. "If you're not in early, you lose any real chance of having an impact on legislation," says Maja Wessels, former chair of AmCham EU and an American with long experience of lobbying Brussels. "Once [a Commission proposal] does see the light of day, it's next to impossible to try and block it," and the opportunities for modification diminish sharply as the proposal moves on through Parliament and the Council.

Even when the latter institutions can modify a proposal, they rarely do so. The drafting process itself involves so much negotiation among directorates and commissioners that the result is, in effect, pretested to withstand the conflicts of ideology and interest which emerge later on. Another key factor is the respect, even deference, which the other institutions show the Commission on account of its expertise. Parliament and the Council do modify legislation, of course, but rarely in fundamental ways.

That's why experienced practitioners agree that the cardinal rule of lobbying in Brussels is: Get In Early. As long as a proposal is a work in progress, at the so-called "internal stage," the Commission is receptive to outside contributions. This is the point at which a company can take a hand in shaping the rules under which it will have to do business. For American companies, which can count on relatively little support from MEPs or national governments, the need to get in early is especially urgent.

Dealing with the Commission: Information, Please

The essential first step is finding out what sort of legislation the Commission is preparing. This can be no simple matter. One big difference between Washington and Brussels, says Ambassador Richard Morningstar, my immediate predecessor as U.S. envoy to the EU, is the openness of the regulatory process. "There's organized transparency in the United States," he notes, referring to the hearings and publications required by the U.S. Administrative Procedure Act, whereas "there's more ad hoc transparency in Europe—depending on the situation, depending on the directorate, depending on who [lobbyists] talk to."

EU lawmaking has become somewhat more open. While preparing its final proposal for the chemicals testing regime called REACH, the Commission solicited comments from all interested parties, including non-EU stakeholders, via the Internet and more traditional media. About 6,000 replies came in, mostly from trade groups, companies, and nongovernmental organizations (NGOs). The Commission responded with changes that it claimed would spare industry billions of euros in costs compared with the previous draft of the proposal.

Though hardly satisfied with the changes, industry took heart from the Commission's handling of the consultation. "All this demonstrates that the willingness is there to become more transparent, to be more accessible," says Jürgen Strube, a board member and former chairman of the German chemicals giant BASF. "And that, in turn, means that lobbying by business becomes also better accepted in the European arena." Maja Wessels agrees that the REACH consultation shows that the EU is "learning and has come to the realization that they do need to be more open, more transparent, and more inclusive" in the legislative process.

Despite increased transparency, information on EU legislation remains inaccessible at the earliest stages, except through informal channels. Not least among these channels, as far as American business goes, is the U.S. mission to the EU. It was the mission that first informed U.S. industry about REACH, shortly after the Commission began work on the proposal; and it was the mission that coordinated an EU-wide campaign for a more business-friendly version of the chemicals regime.

The mission's staff includes representatives of several cabinet departments and agencies, specialists who can help American companies understand how EU policy affects their business. The mission also maintains a website (www.useu.be) with constantly updated information on more than a dozen key issues ranging from agriculture to transportation.

Industry's most important source of knowledge about future EU legislation is the most direct: the Commission staff who actually write the proposals. Lobbyists strive to build relationships with these officials by proving themselves trustworthy providers of information.

The Commission needs information because its human resources do not match its legislative power. Only a few thousand people handle the thousands of regulations, directives, and decisions that the Commission issues every year. As diligent and capable as they are—and a rigorous selection examination ensures that they are both—Commission staff members simply cannot master all the areas on which their work impinges. They depend on the input of stakeholders, including business.

What sort of information do Commission officials want from lobbyists? Research projecting the economic impact of a law can be useful. Chemical companies supplied many such studies on REACH. But it is not only data relating directly to the legislation in question that officials seek; it's anything that can help them understand the industry they are dealing with.

"In some areas, pure statistics are still lacking," notes Dr. Martin Porter, cofounder of a Brussels public affairs consultancy called The Centre. "In, for example, business services sectors, if a company is large enough to have a footprint in all or most European markets, then their statistics can be almost as important as the cobbled-together European version that the Commission is working with."

It's precisely because Commission officials place such importance on solid information that they insist on meeting directly with industry representatives, rather than outside consultants. "I know that officials value the information we have," says Maria Laptev, vice chairman of the lobbying firm GPC Brussels, "but do we always have the answer, the specific answer to that specific question when they're delving a little deeper? Clearly not. It's clearly the client who will have that extra, in-depth answer."

The need for information is even greater among MEPs, particularly those charged with reporting to Parliament's legislative committees. These so-called "rapporteurs" are, along with committee chairmen, the "main gatekeepers in forming the opinion" of Parliament.[3] They lack the staff and other resources to match the Commission in research, so any outside party hoping to influence them must be ready to supply relevant facts and even help with the drafting of Committee reports.

"Lobbyists should be alert to opportunities to make individual rapporteurs 'shine' in the eyes of their colleagues," one lobbyist has written. "Well-crafted legislative reports, based on careful investigation and meticulous analysis, can enhance the reputation of a newly elected MEP. And a reputation for diligence and intellectual acumen can lead to leadership positions in the future."[4] One way to make friends in high places is to help them get there.

Making Their Case

Providing information is just part of the story; the other part is making a convincing case. That may seem obvious, yet American companies don't always seem to understand what persuasion means in a European context.

When CEOs or top managers of U.S. firms come to Brussels to meet with commissioners and other officials, they often arrive primed for conflict. "They go too quickly to the expectation that 'the law says this, and you therefore have to comply,' rather than at least to begin with a slightly softer approach," says Martin Porter. While a hard-hitting style or a legalistic approach can play well in Washington, in Brussels it's apt to make things worse. Diplomacy generally works better.

The drawbacks to playing hardball with the EU were spectacularly clear in the dispute between GE's then-CEO Jack Welch and Mario Monti, the commissioner with the portfolio for antitrust policy until 2004. That confrontation, which ended with the Commission rejecting the GE-Honeywell merger, became highly public and politically charged, with President Bush weighing in on behalf of GE and Commissioner Monti defiantly proclaiming the EU's independence from foreign influence.

Bill Gates has clearly learned from Welch's experience, as we can see in Microsoft's handling of its own antitrust dispute with the Commission. Although the software maker has mounted an aggressive legal challenge to the €497-million fine it received in 2004, and to requirements that it disclose proprietary information and offer alternative versions of its Windows operating system, the company has also worked to offset its image as a monopolistic behemoth. Sponsoring the work of Brussels think tanks has helped in this regard, as has the munificence of the Gates Foundation, the largest philanthropic foundation in the world, with more than $30 billion in assets. The Microsoft chairman himself paid a goodwill visit to Brussels in early 2005, and emerged from a meeting with MEPs to declare: "Anything they want us to do better, I will listen very carefully and make sure we are very responsive."

Attempts at persuasion can backfire when made in inappropriate terms. For instance, business people tend to quantify the economic impact of legislation according to how many jobs will be gained or lost. Since workers are also voters, they reason, such projections are bound to sway politicians. But Commission officials are not politicians in the usual sense, because they are unelected and virtually unaccountable, and so can afford to ignore such warnings.[5]

"There is a distrust [in the Commission] of any organization that simply says, 'if you do that we will have to lose jobs,'" Porter explains, "because there is a view amongst many decision makers that it is being used as an excuse rather than a real problem." Officials assume that businesses "will shed jobs anyway if they need to make sure that their costs get under control"—and that American companies will be especially quick to lay people off.

So which arguments carry the day? Those that take into account the "principles of European integration." A lobbyist in Brussels must invoke not only the ideals of full employment and free trade within the single market, but of "social cohesion"—that is, preservation of the European social model which I discussed in Chapter 3.[6] For many officials, the goal of "competitiveness" (however fashionable that word has become) is secondary to the principle of "corporate social responsibility."

In emphasizing their socially responsible activities, companies must strike a delicate balance between too much publicity—which will provoke the criticism that "it's just PR"—and hiding their light under a bushel. A number of U.S. corporations including Procter & Gamble, Nike, Coca-Cola, and Pfizer have become highly adept at drawing the attention of EU policy makers to their philanthropic contributions. Best of all is when a company can demonstrate the socially responsible ways in which it does business. ExxonMobil, which long sought to keep a low profile in Brussels, has in recent years pursued a strategy of engaging and dispelling environmentalist criticism, for example by emphasizing its excellent safety record and publicizing its efforts to ensure that pipeline projects do not harm the environment. Such efforts do not bring instant results, but over time they build up an invaluable reservoir of good will.

Europeanizing American Business

In their dealings with Brussels, U.S. businesses have certain handicaps, starting with the perceived sins of their government. Commission staff have been known to refuse access to American companies as a way of protesting U.S. policies. A lobbyist specializing in environmental issues for one of the world's largest computer hardware manufacturers, a U.S.-based company which had done nothing to offend the Commission, nevertheless found doors closed to him after Washington failed to ratify the Kyoto Protocol. One Commissioner is said to have snubbed a visiting board member of ExxonMobil in order to register disapproval of the Bush administration's stand on global warming. At such moments, American businesses might regard their country's economic and geopolitical preeminence as less an asset than an albatross.

More commonly, says Martin Porter, American companies "have to overcome the perception that they don't have a significant interest" in Europe's economy and society. They have the burden of proving their "European dimension." One business that has done this well, says Porter, is the Ford Motor Company. Not only are the Detroit auto maker's representatives in Brussels themselves Europeans, they regularly "produce documentation which highlights the ways in which they have a significant European presence: invest heavily in Europe, employ Europeans, export from Europe elsewhere, etc." The company was a major booster of the Delors Commission's drive to complete the single market by 1992. More recently, its executives have spoken openly in favor of Great Britain adopting the common euro currency. Ford has thus earned great credibility as a pro-EU corporation, which certainly helps whenever its executives or lobbyists deal with decision makers in Brussels.

Not all European authorities are equally receptive to such outreach. "If you've got a big facility in Ireland, you can count on Irish support," says Maja Wessels. "In France on the other hand, it's not something that's going to have a real influence on their decision-making." A U.S. firm with operations in Germany might establish a European identity on that basis, she says, but "if your interests are not in line with the interests of a major German company, you're always going to be at a disadvantage."

Commission officials are supposed—indeed, literally sworn—to act not as representatives of their member states but simply as Europeans. Yet national characteristics inevitably survive, not least in attitudes toward Americans. "Frankly, it's a lot easier to work with some nationalities than with others," says one longtime American lobbyist. "You're always happy when you've got a Scandinavian work-ing on an issue, or a Brit, rather than someone from France."

American companies in certain industries, such as aerospace, can expect especially inhospitable treatment. Representatives of Boeing are likely to get a frosty reception from Commission officials, given that firm's fierce rivalry with the EU conglomerate Airbus. Information technology companies, on the other hand, encounter little anti-Americanism from EU officialdom. It's probably no coin-cidence that IT is one industry in which EU reforms have gone far toward creating a free and competitive European market.

At least one European business leader thinks that American companies are in a strong position. "In my opinion the foreign investor in Europe has actually quite a high degree of credibility," says Jürgen Strube, the former BASF chairman. "European institutions are quite willing to listen very, very carefully, I would even say eagerly, to what the foreign investor tells them." For Strube, any difficulty that Americans may have in making their voices heard is less a prob-lem of "credibility or access" than of "networking."

Transatlantic Alliances

One way to hedge against the stigma of Americanness is by making alliances with European industry. Many European trade groups, like the employers' federation UNICE, welcome U.S. firms as members. These groups make it possible for Americans to take part, indirectly, in the expert committees that advise the Commission on long-range policy planning. Individual companies are rarely—in the case of American firms, almost never—invited to sit on these committees, but through the trade associations they can exert influence. U.S. companies can also join issue-specific, ad hoc coalitions like the Packaging Chain Forum, whose leaders include the Coca-Cola Company and Procter & Gamble, and which has taken a big hand in shaping EU policy on packaging waste.

Banding together with European industry is also one way for U.S. companies to influence national governments, since these governments often have ears only for their national firms. It was largely through

European firms and the industry's EU trade group, the European Chemical Industry Council (CEFIC), that the transatlantic chemicals industry persuaded the leaders of Britain, France, and Germany to press the Commission for a more business-friendly version of REACH.[7]

To deal with issues facing business as a whole, beyond specific industries, U.S. companies can join groups such as the Transatlantic Business Dialogue, which brings together CEOs and public officials from both sides of the ocean, and even the European Roundtable of Industrialists.

"Any U.S. corporation with a significant presence in Europe will look at up to four, five, six different avenues in which to pursue their interests," Martin Porter says. AmCham's Susan Danger offers a hypothetical illustration, involving a U.S. auto maker's response to EU environmental regulations: "They'll go to the institutions and say yes or no, 'we think it's great' or 'we want to make this comment.' They'll then work through the [Association of European Automobile Manufacturers], which will say 'we all think x.' Then they'll work through AmCham and the position will come out signed up by a whole range of multisectoral companies. And the strength of it is therefore in the fact that it's not just the car industry saying it, it's the chemical industry, you name it, everybody's signed up."

American companies lobbying Brussels sometimes find themselves, to their surprise, in alliance with public interest groups—or, as Europeans call them, "nongovernmental organizations" (NGOs). These groups "probably have an impact on public opinion which is superior to anything which business or even EU institutions can have on their own," says Strube, who attributes the NGOs' influence to disillusionment with the postwar welfare state and anxiety about globalization.

NGOs are well positioned to present themselves as defenders of "social cohesion." They also enjoy an organizational edge over trade groups and business coalitions, with all the competing interests that such alliances have to balance. In the words of one Brussels lobbyist, NGOs "don't have to get agreement between fifty different companies, they just have to decide that they agree internally and then go for it."

Some NGOs are particularly well plugged into the parliamentary phase of the legislative process. Because almost all MEPs are elected on national slates, rather than by local constituencies (the British delegation being the major exception), they are more susceptible than most elected politicians to pressure from nationally or internationally based nonprofit groups. The European Consumers' Organization (BEUC) and the World Wildlife Fund are especially influential in this sense; many MEPs would not think of drafting resolutions or amendments in those groups' areas of activity without first soliciting their views.

All this adds up to the reality that, as Strube puts it, "business as well as the EU institutions have to consider the NGOs as a very, very important partner in forming policies." Given the hostility to commerce that often marks such groups, corporations may find the thought of partnership less than enticing. But industry and NGOs do have common ground. Aluminum companies, for instance, have worked with European environmentalists to investigate the light-weight metal's energy-saving potential. Maria Laptev, who helped organize that project, observes that NGOs and businesses "do want some of the same things. [The environmentalists] want to make the world a more sustainable place, and the industry has to believe in sustainability, otherwise they're not going to be around."

Cooperation, then, is key to successful lobbying in the EU. Cooperation not just with NGOs and competing businesses, but with the EU institutions themselves. This is hardly surprising when one considers that European integration has been the result, not of conquest by a dominant power, but of compromise and consensus among more than two dozen sovereign nations.

American businesses lobbying Brussels have the added burden of proving their "European dimension." Given the deep trade and investment ties between the U.S. and the EU today, most companies should not find this hard to do. By their very presence in Europe they are taking part in the long transatlantic collaboration—economic as well as political and military—that has made European integration possible.

Notes

1. Bowley, Graham, "Brussels' rise draws lobbyists in numbers," *The International Herald Tribune*, November 18, 2004.

2. The measures in question were the Waste Electrical and Electronic Equipment Directive (WEEE) and the Reduction of Hazardous Substances in Electrical and Electronic Equipment Directive (RoHS).

3. Lehmann, Wilhelm, "Lobbying in the European Union: Current Rules and Practices," European Parliament, April 2003, p. 32.

4. Bulholzer, R. P., *Legislatives Lobbying in der EU*, Bern, 1998, p. 247, cited in Lehmann, p. 35.

5. This is why grassroots campaigning, which aims to influence the Commission by exciting public opinion, is rarely attempted and even less often successful. Campaign contributions, that other potent item in the U.S. lobbyist's toolkit, are for the same reason totally irrelevant when it comes to the Commission. As for parliamentarians, their campaign budgets are by American standards microscopic, and thus so are their needs.

6. Vandenberghe, K., *Lobbying in the European Union*, Government Relations, May 1995, pp. 3–5, cited in Lehmann, p. 20.

7. This transatlantic alliance could have made its own job much easier had it rallied EU member-state governments, particularly the economics and trade ministries, *before* the Commission developed its proposal. By that time, the debate had been framed in terms of environmental protection rather than competitiveness, to the disadvantage of industry. Which goes to show that "getting in early" applies to dealings with the national capitals as well as to Brussels.

Conclusion:
A New Chapter?

I N LATE FEBRUARY 2005, near the end of my tenure as the U.S. ambassador to the European Union, President George W. Bush came to Brussels. The visit was the first foreign trip of his second term, but that was hardly its greatest significance. No U.S. head of state had ever met so extensively with the leaders of the EU institutions in the city where those institutions have their headquarters.

It was all the more meaningful that the president in this case was George W. Bush, whose first term had been marked by severe transatlantic tensions, culminating in the bitter dispute over the Second Gulf War. That ordeal had inspired an impassioned debate in the U.S., both within the administration and among the public, over the proper attitude toward European integration. On one side stood the neoconservatives, who argued that the U.S. could "cherry-pick" European allies by forming coalitions of the willing as it had done for Iraq, thus rendering the EU irrelevant. The realists, among whom I counted myself, insisted on the contrary that European integration was here to stay, that any U.S. policy which could be perceived as one of "divide and conquer" would only spur more furious efforts to unify against it, and that the U.S. should aim instead at confirming our partnership with a united Europe.

When, therefore, President Bush stood before an audience of dignitaries in Brussels to declare that "America supports Europe's democratic unity . . . because freedom leads to peace," and that "America supports a strong Europe, because we need a strong partner in the hard work of advancing freedom and peace in the world," it was clear where he came down in the debate. In fact, from the moment in 2001 when he asked me to serve as his envoy to Brussels, I had never heard him speak in any but friendly and respectful terms about European integration. But during that visit in 2005, the President's remarks both public and private made his position unmistakable to the world. His frequent use of the term "EU" (as distinct from "Europe" or "our European allies") was particularly gratifying to me, as was his obvious respect and willingness to listen when meeting with EU leaders.

"We need all the help and advice we can get," I heard President Bush tell Commission President José Manuel Barroso, adding with specific reference to Israeli-Palestinian peace negotiations: "We've got a shot, but we need the EU with us."

Although he obviously still had personal favorites among the European leaders—I saw him give Italian Prime Minister Silvio Berlusconi a bear hug when the two met outside the headquarters of the Council of Ministers—President Bush was clearly approaching Europe as very much a single entity. On his previous trip to Brussels, nearly four years earlier, the President had visited NATO while bypassing the EU institutions entirely. This time, in an eloquent and highly deliberate bit of symbolism, he spent precisely the same amount of time at both institutions, lending equal importance to the old and new faces of the transatlantic relationship. He also spent as much time with French President Jacques Chirac and other critics as he did with friends such as British Prime Minister Tony Blair.

European reaction to the President's Brussels visit was generally pleased, though restrained by comparison to his reception in post-Communist Slovakia, where later that same week a crowd in Bratislava cheered his call for efforts to promote freedom and democracy around the world. Yet from my perspective "on the ground" in the EU capital, it was striking how eager European politicians were to reconcile with the American president. Luxembourg's Prime Minister Jean-Claude Juncker, whose country held the rotating EU presidency at the time, was besieged by peers seeking "face time" with their U.S. counterpart. Belgium's Prime Minister Guy Verhofstadt, an outspoken critic of the Bush administration's Iraq policy, did not rest until given the job of introducing the President before his speech, tickets for which were the most sought-after commodity in town.

All this reaffirmed my belief that we were indeed beginning a "new era of transatlantic unity," in President Bush's words; or as Secretary of State Condoleeza Rice put it in Paris earlier that same month, a "new chapter in our relationship and a new chapter in our alliance."

As I have argued throughout this book, the prosperity and the security of both Europe and America depend on our overcoming the disputes of recent years. The costs of damage to our $2.5-trillion annual commercial relationship, and the danger in a breakdown of the Atlantic alliance, are grim to contemplate, not only for the populations of the U.S. and the EU but for the rest of the world as well. A global regulatory regime driven by a dirigiste EU would hamper innovation and growth everywhere. A Euro-Gaullist EU bent on establishing itself as an alternative geopolitical "pole" to the U.S. could undermine stability all around the globe. On the other hand, the opportunities for cooperation in ways beneficial to both our societies and to all humankind make transatlantic harmony a moral as well as a strategic imperative.

Making that imperative all the more urgent is the fleeting nature of the opportunity. At the moment, America is unchallenged as the world's sole military superpower. The tightly interlinked U.S. and EU economies account for 41 percent of world GDP, 27 percent of world exports, 32 percent of world imports, and 77 percent of foreign direct investment in the rest of the world.[1] But China and India have much faster-growing economies and are developing military capabilities and geostrategic ambitions to match. These vast countries, already major powers in their regions, could join the ranks of global powers in as little as two decades.

The rise of these Asian giants is not necessarily inimical to the interests and values of America and Europe. As the world's largest democracy, India could emerge as a magnificent force for global development and stability. Encouraging China's transition to democracy and the rule of law should be the common project of all free nations. But a world in which Washington must listen to Beijing and New Delhi as attentively as to London, Paris, Berlin, or Moscow will require an entirely new set of geostrategic calculations. We cannot know with any precision what Europe and America will be able to accomplish, or how we will be required to act, in that brave new world. The only agenda we can make today is the one which we must act on now.

Certain goals stand out as especially urgent.

In the Middle East, the U.S. and the EU together can effectively press for a settlement to the Palestinian-Israeli conflict and can help manage the establishment of an independent Palestinian state that will coexist peacefully with its neighbor. In Iraq, we must leave behind our disagreements and collaborate in military and nonmilitary ways to ensure a stable democracy. A major step toward this goal was the June 2005 conference in Brussels, where Secretary Rice met with her EU counterparts to coordinate multilateral assistance for Iraq's reconstruction and political transition. Across the Middle East, Europe and America should work to promote democratic reform, the foundation of long-term stability and the surest bulwark against extremism and terrorism.

In Africa and other underdeveloped regions, America and Europe share the power and the duty to alleviate suffering and to help build societies able to help themselves. We can do this through development assistance linked to political and economic reforms, but also by spreading the benefits of free trade, through the agenda laid out in the World Trade Organization's "Doha Round" of negotiations.

Although NATO remains the bedrock of America's security relationship with Europe, the U.S. must develop a security relationship with the EU itself, to parallel our growing political dialogue. Along with coordinated programs of humanitarian and development assistance, cooperation between the U.S. and the EU in peacekeeping, nation-building, and crisis prevention would make us an unparalleled joint force for global stability, ready to intervene in crises and potential crises around the world, to help establish the conditions for democracy and economic freedom.

By closely coordinating our intelligence and law enforcement operations against terrorism, the U.S. and the EU could make both continents safer while reducing one of the major obstacles to peace in the Middle East. In an age of global organized crime, such cooperation could also curtail the scope for drug running, money laundering, traffic in human beings, and other forms of social corruption.

We must address the challenges of global climate change. Although we disagree over the particular approach codified in the Kyoto Protocol, we agree on the need to reduce dangerous emissions, and there is much Europe and America can do together in the field of research to set the stage for environmentally sound growth.

A Barrier-Free Transatlantic Marketplace (BFTM) would make Europe and America more prosperous through the elimination of all remaining barriers to competition in goods, capital, and services, including tariffs that now average 3–4 percent on the $500 billion of annual U.S.-EU trade. Just as NAFTA has successfully joined countries as politically and economically different as Canada, Mexico, and the U.S., each with laws and regulations that suit its particular priorities and needs, so a BFTM could bring together the U.S. and the EU to our common benefit, while allowing us to pursue our diverse models of social organization.

The U.S. Congress and the EU institutions should establish closer cooperation, and an "early warning system" to alert each side whenever the other contemplates rules that would affect us both. A common procedure for assessing the economic impact of proposed regulation would be a logical outgrowth of such cooperation.

Our societies would also benefit from a more general willingness to learn from each other's successes and adopt each other's best practices. Americans observing European ways could gain a keener appreciation of quality of life, leisure, and family time, as goods to balance against material well-being. Europe, the society that invented capitalism, could draw inspiration from American examples of initiative, risk-taking, and entrepreneurship. The Old World could also look at America's long history of assimilating diverse ethnic groups, for lessons to apply in Europe's approach to immigration.

To do all this, we need a new generation of Americans and Europeans invested in the transatlantic relationship: a cadre of people in government, business, academia, think tanks, the press, and other professions who understand how both systems work and how they can deal with each other.

In this department, I am afraid to say, Americans have a lot of catching up to do. Europeans think, read, and hear about the U.S. all the time. Of course, the information they get is not always accurate, and the interpretations to which they are exposed are not always fair. Certainly there is room for improvement in our public diplomacy, to make sure that the U.S. side of the story gets heard. But at least we know the audience is there. By contrast, American awareness of Europe is dim. Our schools and universities teach European history and culture much less than they used to, and they teach hardly at all about the political and economic reality of European integration. Except when it comes to trade issues, the American press ignores the EU. Only one major U.S. news organization, *The Wall Street Journal*, maintains a permanent presence in Brussels. My hope is that a greater focus on the EU by our political and business leaders will lead academics and journalists to pay more attention.

This short list is a tall order, I know. But we have the resources to accomplish it all and far more. Not only do our common interests point toward greater cooperation and mutual awareness, our values do as well.

As President Bush said in Brussels: "For more than sixty years, our nations stood together to face great challenges of history. Together, we opposed totalitarian ideologies with our might and with our patience. Together, we united this continent with our democratic values. And together we mark, year by year, the anniversaries of freedom—from D-Day, to the liberation of death camps, to the victories of conscience in 1989."

This is the basis on which the U.S. and the EU can work together to spread prosperity and freedom around the world. Whether or not the EU fulfills its potential as a superpower in every respect, it remains our natural and indispensable partner. In Simon Serfaty's formulation, Europe and America constitute a community of interests and values, which it is our challenge to transform into a community of action. I hope that this book will be a small contribution toward that end.[2]

Notes

1. Hamilton, Daniel S., and Joseph P. Quinlan, *Partners in Prosperity: The Changing Geography of the Transatlantic Economy*, Washington, D.C.: Center for Transatlantic Relations, 2004, p. 177.

2. See, generally, Simon Serfaty, *The Vital Partnership: Power and Order, America and Europe Beyond Iraq*, Lanham, Md.: Rowman & Littlefield, 2005.

———— ❦ ————

The European Union Institutions

W ITH THEIR FREQUENTLY similar names and shared "competences" (Brussels jargon for authority in a given field), the institutions of the European Union form a confusing structure typically described as a labyrinth. Although the EU is rooted in the same broad parliamentary tradition as liberal democracies around the world, including the United States, it is a unique amalgam of elements, formed over half a century to serve diverse and sometimes conflicting organizational visions. Attempts to plug the EU into other existing constitutional models—for instance by equating the Commission with the White House, Parliament with the U.S. Congress, and so forth—immediately break down, leaving the observer bewildered. What's more, the institutions themselves and the relationships among them are still changing. Here I offer a general picture of the major institutions, concentrating on basic features unlikely to change in the near future. This survey takes the form of a tour, following the progress of a hypothetical piece of legislation from the initial idea to its enforcement as EU law.

A ll EU law officially begins its life in the European Commission, which has the sole "right of initiative" to propose legislation. Its main offices are housed in a star-shaped high-rise in Brussels called the Berlaymont, built on the former site of a convent of Augustinian nuns, "les Dames du Berlaymont." The Commission employs only about 24,000 people total, a fact often cited to debunk myths of an all-powerful Brussels bureaucracy. However, the institution wields influence far out of proportion to its size, largely because the laws that it produces are implemented by other institutions—that is, the governments of the EU member states. The Commission is divided for administrative purposes into thirty-seven directorates-general, twenty-three of which are responsible for policy and legislation, the rest being devoted to administrative matters such as accounting and translation.

The Commission's civil service at the higher levels is chosen by a rigorous competitive examination called a *concours*, which requires in-depth knowledge not only of EU law and administration, but also of European politics, economics, history, and culture. Many of the most successful Commission staff members are also graduates of the elite College of Europe in Bruges, Belgium, which offers a one-year master's course in European studies, and whose graduates are said to form a "Bruges Mafia" throughout the EU institutions and among private-sector lobbyists in Brussels. Commission staff are expected to serve in the "general interest of the Community" and lay aside national allegiances during their employment there, a commitment reinforced by unofficial etiquette that discourages overt identification with any particular member state. For instance, instead of saying "my country," a Commission staff member is more likely to refer to "the country I know best." By all accounts, most of these people sincerely embrace the supranational ideals of the EU project, which is why they have come to work there in the first place. There are material compensations, too: a virtually untaxed salary, an allowance for children's schooling, subsidized travel to one's home country, and a generous pension. All this, in one of Western Europe's least expensive and most livable (though also one of its rainiest) capitals.

Let's imagine one of these staffers working in the (fictional) Gizmo Unit of the (fictional) Directorate-General for Gadgets, which we'll call DG Gadgets. This enterprising young official conceives of a single EU safety standard for a subclass of gizmos which we'll call widgets. He consults with his immediate colleagues, incorporates their suggestions, and presents the idea to his head of unit, who gives the go-ahead. Once other units within the same subdirectorate have made their comments, and the officials in charge of widget regulation in all twenty-five member states have made theirs, the head of the Gizmo Unit passes up a modified version of the proposal to the subdirector.

At this stage, other subdirectorates within DG Gadgets which might have an interest also get a look, and if no one presents an insuperable impediment, the evolving proposal eventually comes before the director-general. By now, it will also have come under the scrutiny of at least one expert committee. These committees, which number more than a thousand (there is no official count), include researchers as well as representatives of the business and nonprofit worlds. They are not strictly speaking part of the legislative process, but since they are personally appointed by the commissioners and directors-general, they have great influence on the shape and eventual survival of any proposal.

Before the director-general passes the widget legislation up to his commissioner, other DGs also get their licks in. (As you might suspect, the progression is not as neatly pyramidal as I am making it sound. DG Research, for instance, is likely to be consulted for technical input quite early in the process. But this should convey the general dynamic and hierarchy of decision-making.) Public hearings must also be held to get the views of stakeholders, including widget manufacturers, consumer groups, labor unions, and ordinary citizens with an interest in the subject. After a period that can stretch to years from the time the young staff member first conceived of new widget safety standards, the proposal is presented to the commissioner whose portfolio includes DG Gadgets.

There are twenty-five members of the College of Commissioners, one from each member state, serving a term of five years. Commissioners are typically prominent politicians or former cabinet ministers in their home countries, in some cases nearing the end of their careers, in other cases with prospects still bright.[1] Though the commissioners take an oath to serve the "general interest of the Community" while in office, considerations of national politics have been known to play a role in their actions. For instance, British commissioners lobbied heavily for many years so that their country would receive an annual rebate on its contributions to the EU budget, an abatement worth $4.8 billion per year to British taxpayers by 2005.

Because there are more directorates-general than there are seats on the Commission, some commissioners are responsible for more than one DG. Decisions as to who does what are up to the Commission's president. Unlike the other twenty-four members, selected by their national governments, the president of the Commission is chosen by all the member-state governments together in the European Council (see below). Since November 2004, the presidency has been occupied by José Manuel Barroso, a former prime minister of Portugal. The Barroso Commission is generally more economically liberal and Atlanticist than its predecessor, a reflection of the center-right's dominance of European politics in 2004. President Barroso assigned the two most powerful directorates-general, for trade negotiation and antitrust enforcement, to politicians known for their pro-business views: Britain's Peter Mandelson and Neelie Kroes of the Netherlands.

The College of Commissioners meets around a large oval table on the top floor of the thirteen-story Berlaymont. Decisions are strictly speaking by majority vote, but since the smooth functioning of the Commission requires a high degree of consensus, a successful president must have strong leadership skills as well as a flair for making deals.

Now that the Commission has approved our directive for uniform widget safety standards, the proposal travels to the European Parliament, housed in a vast glass building less than half a mile from the Berlaymont.

Parliament has 732 members, elected by citizens of the twenty-five member states in rough proportion to population, though the vast discrepancies in national size mean that there is only one member for every 830,000 Germans, but five for the 400,000 citizens of Malta. Because most countries elect their members (known as MEPs) on national slates by the method of proportional representation, even small parties with scattered support can win seats. The current Parliament thus includes over 150 different parties, of almost every conceivable persuasion ranging from unreconstructed Communists to neofascists. The 2004 elections were notable for the debut, with eleven seats, of the United Kingdom Independence Party, a Euroskeptic group whose stated goal is to withdraw Britain from the EU. Those same elections were marked by the worst voter turnout in Parliament's history, 45.3 percent on average and just 26.4 percent in the newest member states. A mere 17 percent of Slovakians took advantage of their first opportunity to cast ballots for MEPs.

For practical purposes, the parties in Parliament have formed themselves into seven major groups, which caucus and generally vote together. The largest of these, with just under 300 members, is the European People's Party (EPP), made up mostly of parties identifying themselves as "Christian Democrats." In 2004, the EPP struck a deal with the Socialists, the second largest group with about 235 members, whereby the Spanish Socialist Josep Borrell would serve as president of Parliament until the end of 2006, halfway through the current term, whereupon he would hand over the office to someone from the EPP (probably its leader, Hans-Gert Poettering of Germany). The size of a parliamentary group determines the amount of speaking time its MEPs get when addressing the floor, and the number of seats it receives on the various legislative committees.

MEPs are paid the same salary as members of parliament in their home countries, with the result that an Italian receives some €132,000 a year, while a Hungarian must make do with €9,200 for the same job. However, all receive the same living allowance of €262 per day whenever they are in Brussels or Strasbourg, as well as reimbursement for travel expenses.[2] They also receive the same resources for work: a two-room office suite and allowance for a personal staff of up to four persons (though they can choose to pay the entire allowance to one). MEPs can hire anyone they wish for their personal staff, and many choose their spouses or relatives. Additional staff are assigned to the political groups in proportion to their size. The largest group, the EPP, has about 200 such staff members distributed among the various committees.

In plenary sessions and committee meetings, MEPs may choose to speak in their native tongue, while nonspeakers listen through headphones to translations provided by simultaneous interpreters.[3] An even bigger practical challenge is that presented by the monthly trip back and forth to Parliament's other seat in Strasbourg, France. Twelve times a year, the MEPs and more than 1,000 staff members travel 280 miles to the city just across the Rhine from Germany, a location symbolic of the Franco-German reconciliation with which the EU began. There the MEPs hold four days of plenary sessions in a building completed in 1999 at a cost of $400 million. The monthly move, which itself costs €160 million a year by official estimates, and €200 million according to a group of MEPs who favor ending the practice, was a concession by member-state governments to France's President François Mitterrand in 1992. Parliament voted in 2004 to abolish the Strasbourg sessions and meet only in Brussels, but it has no power to decide the issue. Any change would require that the member states amend their agreement.

Strangely for a lawmaking body, Parliament has no right to *propose* legislation, yet it can make significant amendments, and its committees increasingly provide the impetus for legislation officially formulated in the Commission. Long an assembly with merely consultative powers, Parliament has grown increasingly important since the introduction in 1992 of the "co-decision" process, which effectively gives it the ability to veto legislation in several areas, mostly having to do with the single market. Under the 2004 constitutional treaty, Parliament would also have significant powers in the area of law enforcement. The legislature can veto the European Commission's €100-billion annual budget.

Parliament's most dramatic assertions of power have been over the personnel and standing of the Commission itself. In 1999, following an official report of widespread corruption in the Commission under President Jacques Santer, parliamentary pressure contributed to the decision by the entire College of Commissioners to resign. Five years later, Parliament forced two designated members on the Barroso Commission's original slate to withdraw, and another to take a different portfolio than what the President had originally intended.

Ordinarily, however, Parliament is occupied with more mundane concerns like our proposed widget directive. Such a proposal is first considered in the appropriate committee, whose findings, including any suggested amendments, are summarized and presented to the rest of Parliament by the Committee's rapporteur (reporter), a role with greater influence than the name might suggest. The legislation may then be debated in plenary session, although "debate" is hardly the word for the series of short statements, with no opportunity for reply, that is the norm on the floor of the plenary chamber.

All of this constitutes what is known as "first reading." Parliament must go through the same process again, called "second reading," before actually voting. In the meantime, the proposal has also been under consideration by the most powerful EU institution of them all.

Across the street from the Commission's headquarters in the Berlaymont sits the Justus Lipsius Building, named for a sixteenth-century Flemish humanist and political philosopher. In this building we find the main offices of the Council of the European Union (also known as the Council of Ministers), the institution through which the member states act collectively as the EU's top decision-making body.

The Council is actually nine separate councils, each composed of cabinet ministers with equivalent portfolios from the twenty-five member states. The most important formation, made up of foreign ministers, is called General Affairs and External Relations Council (Gaerc). Economics and finance ministers come together in the formation known as "Ecofin." Justice and interior ministers meet in the Justice and Home Affairs Council. The various formations meet regularly throughout the year to consider and vote on legislation in their given areas.

At least twice a year, the heads of state or government of the twenty-five member states meet in a formation known as the European Council, to decide matters of the greatest import for the EU as a whole and to set its general direction.[4] Under current arrangements, the presidency of the European Council is held for six months by each member state on a rotating basis. But under the constitutional treaty, the European Council would instead choose a single person to serve as president for two and a half years. The constitutional treaty would also introduce an EU foreign minister, chosen by the European Council, who would sit on both the Council and the College of Commissioners, thus bridging the intergovernmental and supranational branches of the EU's governing structure. Even with the constitution unratified by the member states, the Council could still choose to institute the offices of EU president and foreign minister.

Because the ministers necessarily spend most of their time in their respective national capitals, the majority of Council work is actually prepared for them by the Committee of Permanent Representatives, known as Coreper (pronounced "Co-repair"), made up of ambassadors from the twenty-five member states. There are actually three sets of permanent representatives, all of ambassadorial rank, with responsibility for different aspects of the Council's work: Coreper I, which deals primarily with social and economic matters; Coreper II, which handles foreign policy, political, and financial matters; and the Political and Security Committee, which concentrates on defense matters. (Coreper II is the most senior body, made up of heads of mission, while members of the PSC are the most junior.) These three committees do most of the actual discussing and negotiating on behalf of their superiors in the member-state capitals. As such, they are extremely influential on the EU-related policies of their governments.

After all the preparation by permanent representatives, the most intractable disagreements among the member states are left for the Council members themselves to work out. This they do in meetings which are closed to all public and press, and whose minutes are never published, and which are thus excellent opportunities for horse-trading, even at the highest levels. In a now-famous, leaked exchange at a 2001 meeting of the European Council, Italian Prime Minister Silvio Berlusconi argued for establishing the European Food Safety Authority in Parma, Italy, rather than Helsinki, Finland, with the claim: "Parma is synonymous with good cuisine. The Finns don't even know what prosciutto is." The Prime Minister of Sweden, Goran Persson, complained that Spain, rather than his country, had received the EU's information technology security agency, prompting French President Jacques Chirac to suggest: "How would it be if Sweden got an agency for training models, since you have such pretty women?" (The Food Safety Authority was eventually located in Parma after all.)

Most council decisions are made by qualified majority voting (QMV), a method whereby member states' votes are weighted according to a complicated formula based largely, but not exactly, on population. Under the simpler "double majority" method in the 2004 constitutional treaty, a proposal would carry if it won the votes of at least 55 percent of the member states with at least 65 percent of the EU's total population. By preventing small states from blocking legislation on their own, this formula would presumably reduce what Americans call "legislative gridlock." Certain sensitive areas of legislation, however, would continue to require unanimous voting. One of these areas is fiscal policy, and as long as this remains the case, efforts to establish common tax rates for EU nations are bound to fail.

Our widget standards proposal would certainly be decided by QMV. Let's assume that it is not so controversial that any difficulties cannot be worked out in Coreper I, which then presents a slightly modified version of the proposal for the approval of the Employment, Social Policy, Health and Consumer Affairs Council (since widget safety standards fall under the rubric of consumer protection). This constitutes the Council's first reading of the legislation. Parliament then goes through its second reading and the Council follows suit. Finally the two bodies vote, and the legislation passes.

Just because the EU's legislative process has passed a proposal into law doesn't mean that our story is done. That would be too simple! The law needs to be implemented, and for that purpose we return to the Commission, now acting in its capacity as the EU's executive branch.

First, some more Brussels jargon. Our widget law is what is known as a "directive," one of the EU's two major types of "legal instrument." The other major legal instrument is called a "regulation." The difference between the two is that a regulation applies immediately throughout the EU, whereas a directive is implemented indirectly through the member states, meaning that twenty-five national systems need to pass laws enforcing it, through a process known as "transposition." Since the Commission prefers not to impose laws directly onto the member states, most EU law is in the form of directives.

Because transposition is a complicated business, with all too much room for divergence in interpretation, the Commission produces detailed guidelines for the member states to follow in passing the necessary laws. But the Commission cannot simply tell the states what to do. Its draft guidelines come under the collective scrutiny of all the member states through the so-called "comitology" process. There are about 350 comitology committees, made up of one representative from each of the member states, with a member of the Commission civil service as chairman. These committees approve or modify the Commission's proposals for implementation, which then go to the member state capitals, so that directives can finally take effect.

You might suppose, given all the opportunities that the member states have had to scrutinize and modify our widget directive before Brussels was done with it, that by this point passing the necessary national laws would be virtually automatic. Yet all the EU countries suffer from a "transposition deficit": a backlog of Commission directives that are yet to be reflected in their own statutes. In early 2005, more than 25 percent of directives pertaining to the single market had still not been transposed in at least one country.

Let's imagine that all twenty-five member states—except one—transpose our widget directive into law. The delinquent government shows no sign of taking the required action. Maybe that's because its local manufacturers do a large trade in low-quality widgets for the non-EU market, and these companies have pressured the government not to saddle them with the more costly standards. But along comes an entrepreneur in that country who sells higher-quality widgets, largely to customers in other EU member states. She has no choice but to meet the new uniform standards. Wanting her local competitors to take on the same regulatory burden, she complains to her national government, which gives her no satisfaction. So she appeals to the Commission.

If an EU member state does not fulfill its obligations, the Commission can take the national authorities to the European Court of Justice (ECJ), the final arbiter of disputes under EU law, and the highest authority on that law's interpretation.[5] The ECJ is made up of twenty-five judges, one from each member state, who hold their sessions in Luxembourg, about 130 miles from Brussels. The Court's powers have gradually expanded since its founding in 1952. Among its most significant decisions has been to uphold the rights of EU citizens to receive state-sponsored medical care in any of the member states, making it possible for Europeans to "shop" for this all-important benefit across the continent. Thus, a Briton who needs a specialized form of surgery more readily available in France can receive it there on the same terms as a French citizen—that is, without paying a fee.

The ECJ's docket had become so crowded that in 1987 the member states established a lower tribunal, the Court of First Instance (CFI), to take on lesser cases such as employment disputes involving EU employees. Since then, the lower court's jurisdiction has grown wider. In late 2004, the CFI made news when it denied a request by Microsoft Corporation to postpone payment of a €497-million fine imposed by the Commission for antitrust violations. The CFI also required Microsoft to comply at once with the Commission's order to modify its Windows operating system and share proprietary information with competitors. Final judgment on Microsoft's case will come from the ECJ.

If the ECJ rules that a member state has not fulfilled its duties— for instance, by failing to transpose our widget directive into its national law—and the member state *still* does not comply, then the Commission can send a "reasoned opinion" to the delinquent national authorities urging them to do so. If *that* fails, the Commission can return to the Court seeking to punish the member state with fines. This has happened exactly once, in 2000, when the Court fined Greece €20,000 per day for failing to stop the illegal dumping of hazardous waste. The process had taken twelve years from the time of the initial complaint, and Greece finally shut down the offending dump in 2003.

Political reality does not always line up with the language of treaties, and the reality is that EU member states, especially the biggest ones, still have plenty of power with which to flout supranational authority. We saw this clearly in 2003, when the Commission stood by helplessly as France and Germany, unapologetically and with the sanction of most fellow member states, violated prescribed limits on their budget deficits, which are an essential part of the fiscal policy underpinning the euro. Although the ECJ ruled the following year that the Council had acted illegally in suspending the Growth and Stability Pact, no fine was imposed; and the Commission was forced to devise a laxer version of the Pact.

Let's suppose that the recalcitrant member state, whether or not under threat of a fine, finally transposes the widget directive into national law. Now that the playing field is even, can our entrepreneur get back to thinking about widgets and forget all about the EU institutions? Not necessarily. If she is based in one of the member states that use the euro (twelve countries to date, with several more hoping to join in the next decade), her export business will be deeply affected by the policies of the European Central Bank.

The ECB is based in Frankfurt, Germany, which is no accident, since the deutsche mark was by far the strongest of the continental European currencies subsumed in the euro. The Bank is governed by an eighteen-member council, consisting of the central bank governors from the twelve euro zone countries, plus an executive board of six, including the president, chosen by the member states. Jean-Claude Trichet, former head of the French central bank, began an eight-year term as president in 2003.

The ECB is the euro zone's equivalent of the U.S. Federal Reserve, but unlike the Fed, it does not gear its policies to measures of economic activity such as unemployment and inflation rates with the aim of promoting growth. In the German tradition of avoiding inflation at all costs (a legacy of the hyperinflation that battered the post–World War I Weimar Republic and helped make possible the rise of Hitler), the ECB has in its first several years established a policy of steady interest rates and of resisting intervention in the international currency markets to affect the exchange value of the euro. As the euro's rise against the dollar began to make painful dents in European exports in 2004, some euro-zone governments, particularly Germany, agitated publicly in favor of intervention; but as of this writing the ECB has not backed down.

Thus our entrepreneur, like every EU citizen and millions of others around the world, increasingly finds her daily life shaped by the decisions and actions of the EU institutions.

Notes

1. Two members of the Prodi Commission (1999–2004) left office before their terms were up to take major cabinet posts in the governments of France and Spain. The President himself, Romano Prodi, a former Prime Minister of Italy, openly backed center-left candidates in his home country's elections for the European Parliament while he was still in office in Brussels and is widely considered a candidate for the Italian premiership in 2006.

2. In 2004, an Austrian MEP named Hans-Peter Martin produced videotaped evidence that his colleagues were routinely claiming travel and expense allowances without attending sessions of Parliament. He was kicked off the Socialist ticket, but ran as an independent and was reelected with 14 percent of his nation's vote.

3. Providing direct simultaneous interpretation for every possible combination of the EU's twenty official languages would require as many as 380 interpreters on duty all at once, an unrealistic proposition particularly given the rarity of certain tongues. There are, for instance, only eight qualified Maltese translators available to serve all of the EU institutions. English therefore commonly serves as an intermediate language, so that, for example, Estonian and Maltese interpreters both work from the English translation of a speech actually delivered in Portuguese. Since the interpreting is supposed to be *simultaneous*, that makes for quite a relay race. A Parliament official assures me that misunderstandings are nonetheless rare.

4. The European Council should not be confused with either the Council of the European Union (of which it is a part) or the Council of Europe, a completely separate intergovernmental organization based in Strasbourg, France. Founded in 1949, the Council of Europe was an important inspiration for the EU, and with forty-six member states today, it remains especially active in promoting democracy, human rights, and the rule of law.

5. The European Court of Justice is not to be confused with the European Court of Human Rights, which is not an EU institution and is affiliated with the Council of Europe. Operating in Strasbourg, France, the Court of Human Rights enforces the European Convention on Human Rights, drawn up in 1950, to which all EU member states are signatories.

———— ⌁ ————

The European Union
Member States

THE EUROPEAN UNION is made up of twenty-five sovereign nations, each with its own geopolitical orientation and prevailing economic philosophy. During my tenure as ambassador, I visited them all at least once, an experience which immeasurably enhanced my understanding of the EU institutions in Brussels. Since it is the national governments that ultimately determine the EU's laws and policies, considering the member states as individuals is indispensable to comprehending the Union as a whole.

Yet the nations of Europe are not atomized units but parts of a complex social, cultural, and economic organism. To highlight the links as well the differences among them, this appendix considers the EU's twenty-five members, and four candidate states, in regional terms, listing only two of them as individual countries. I have also included the four members of the European Free Trade Association (EFTA) as a group, since for this book's purposes what these nations have in common is their decision not to join the EU.

My approach in this survey is emphatically *not* scientific, but based on my personal impressions. Those looking for an authoritative source of basic information on the EU, or any other countries, should consult *The World Factbook*, published annually by the CIA and

updated throughout the year, on the Internet at http://www.cia.gov/
cia/publications/factbook/.

Much of the economic information in this chapter is drawn from
The Index of Economic Freedom, published by the Heritage Foundation
and the *Wall Street Journal*, on the Internet at http://www.heritage
.org/research/features/index/.

Baltic States: Estonia, Latvia, Lithuania
Benelux: Belgium, the Netherlands, Luxembourg
British Isles: Great Britain, Republic of Ireland
Bulgaria and Romania (candidates)
Central Europe: Austria, Croatia (candidate), the Czech Republic,
   Hungary, Slovakia, Slovenia
European Free Trade Association (not EU members): Iceland,
   Liechtenstein, Norway, Switzerland
France and Germany
Greece and Cyprus
Iberia: Spain, Portugal
Italy and Malta
Poland
Scandinavia: Denmark, Finland, Sweden
Turkey (candidate)

BALTIC STATES

Estonia, Latvia, Lithuania

With their distinct cultural heritages, these proud nations bristle at
being lumped together as "the Baltics." Lithuania, for instance, is pri-
marily Roman Catholic, whereas the other two nations have large
Lutheran and Orthodox communities. However, the three countries do
share a number of important characteristics, including close and long-
standing ties to neighboring Scandinavia. More than half of Estonia's
exports go to Sweden and Finland, and all the major banks in Lithuania
are Scandinavian-based. As former Soviet republics, the Baltic states
also share important interests and problems with the other post-
Communist states that joined the EU in 2004. Like those countries, the
Baltic states are still working to create transparent and efficient pub-

lic institutions. Their experience as Soviet vassals makes them especially sensitive to political developments in Russia and especially appreciative of the U.S. as the ultimate guarantor of their security.

Economic Policy

When I visited Estonia in 2005, a successful businessman there told me that it took him only eight minutes every year to fill out his income tax form, which he, like 65 percent of the population, filed electronically. This reflects not only the country's embrace of the information economy—I saw wireless Internet hot spots everywhere I went—but also its fair and simple tax policies. Estonia has led its region in lowering taxes, cutting the public budget, privatizing state-owned industry, and reducing regulations that affect commerce. A zero percent corporate tax on all profits reinvested in the country has earned Estonia the nickname "the Delaware of Europe." Neighboring Finland has already responded to the competition by lowering its tax on alcoholic spirits and is planning to cut other taxes. The only major exception to Estonia's free economic policies is its price controls on a wide range of goods, from electricity to tobacco.

Latvia and Lithuania have been following Estonia's liberalizing lead, only more slowly. Both countries are still seriously troubled by burdensome regulations, inefficient courts, government corruption, and organized crime. Lithuania takes up the rear of the group with regard to privatization, though its sophisticated community of young entrepreneurs will no doubt speed that process as they gain greater influence.

Though these countries continue to exert competitive pressure on the senior EU member states to their west, they are increasingly worried about losing jobs to nonmembers Belarus and Ukraine, which can offer industry even lower wages.

Relations with the U.S.

Leaders of all three countries signed the "Vilnius Group" letter in February of 2003 supporting U.S. policy toward Saddam Hussein. The countries all contributed troops to the coalition in Iraq and joined NATO in 2004. Latvia in particular has a Euroatlanticist orientation reinforced by its population of North American "re-émigrés," people of Latvian birth or origin who have returned since the fall of Communism to rebuild their country, exemplified by President Vaira Vike-Freiberga, a former professor of psychology at the University of Montreal. Some of Latvia's many international banks—about twenty in a country of only 2.3 million people—have been linked to money-laundering operations, an issue of increasing concern to Washington.

BENELUX

Belgium, the Netherlands, Luxembourg

These three small countries, all of which numbered among the six founding member states of the European Coal and Steel Community in 1951, share a historic commitment to European integration. Their traditional enthusiasm for the EU reflects centuries of common experience as a focal point of conflict between the major European powers, especially France and Germany. European integration has given the Benelux nations protection against their larger neighbors and allowed them to wield influence far out of proportion to their size. Despite all they have in common, the Benelux countries are a strikingly diverse group with regard to both economic philosophy and geopolitical orientation.

Belgium is culturally divided between the Dutch-speaking region of Flanders and the French-speaking region of Wallonia. Though the Walloons long supplied the country's ruling class, the Flemings in more recent generations have emerged as the more entrepreneurial and successful community. The right-wing Flemish party Vlaams Belang has garnered increasing support with a policy opposing Muslim immigration.

The Netherlands has a long tradition of tolerance and compromise, exemplified by its "Polder model" of consensus among unions, employers, and the government and its liberal social mores regarding sexuality and drug use. However, in the wake of violence by Islamist militants, the Dutch have recently been rethinking their multicultural approach to ethnic relations, and some prominent voices have even called for an end to non-Western immigration. Dutch voters' rejection of the proposed constitution bespeaks discontent with aspects of today's EU, including the Netherlands' disproportionate contribution to the EU budget and the prospective accession of Turkey; but the ideal of European integration is, I am convinced, still popular among my former compatriots.

Economic Policy

Luxembourg, with the world's highest per capita GDP, is also one of the world's freest economies, since its largest industry, financial services, is subject to little government regulation. Only in 2005, under pressure from other EU member states, did Luxembourg begin withholding tax on accounts held by nonresidents. Its banking secrecy laws remain in force for now. Luxembourg's top corporate tax rate is 22.9 percent.

By contrast, neighboring Belgium suffers under what the *Index of Economic Freedom* calls "one of Western Europe's most punishing tax systems and one of the world's highest total tax burdens." Belgian employers must contend with high wages and social contributions, Byzantine health and safety requirements, and strict limits on firing. Price controls exist for a wide range of goods, even for some kinds of automobiles and bread. Government permission can be necessary to introduce a new product on the market. Not surprisingly, with so many regulations, the Belgian bureaucracy and judiciary are by Northern European standards sluggish.

Like the Belgians, the Dutch have a tradition of seeking consensus among employers, labor unions, and the government. The difference is that in the Netherlands this process has led in recent years to significant cuts in state spending, lower wages, and more flexible labor markets. My native land lives up to its heritage as a great trading nation, thanks largely to an almost total lack of barriers to foreign investment. Its financial industry is only lightly regulated. Taxes are still too high, but it is now a lot easier to fire workers in the Netherlands—and thus to hire them—than it is in Germany or France.

Relations with the U.S.

Though all three countries were among the founding members of NATO in 1949, the transatlantic crisis over Iraq revealed significant differences in their attitudes toward the U.S.

In February 2003, Belgium joined France and Germany in opposing security guarantees for NATO member Turkey against any reprisals for a U.S.-led invasion of Iraq. It was this vote that prompted Secretary of State Powell to warn that the "the alliance is breaking itself up because it will not meet its responsibilities." A few months later, Belgium and Luxembourg joined France and Germany in calling for an EU military planning headquarters separate from the NATO command structure.

The Netherlands, by contrast, is a strong supporter of NATO's integrity and contributed one of the larger contingents of troops for the occupation of Iraq.

History and geography help to explain these countries' different orientations. Belgium's proximity to France, and particularly to the capital of that highly centralized state, and the fact that Belgium's ruling class has been traditionally drawn from the Francophone Walloon community have made the Kingdom of Belgium a political and cultural satellite of its powerful neighbor.

The Grand Duchy of Luxembourg, caught as it is between France and Germany, has often had to strike a balance between the interests of those two large nations. When Paris and Berlin manage to agree, as they did over Iraq, it is only natural that Luxembourg will go along.

In the case of the Netherlands, contiguity has produced not affinity but enduring suspicion. There are still many Dutch who personally remember the horrific ordeal of Nazi occupation during World War II. While Germany is obviously not a military threat today, continuing apprehension toward it helps drive Dutch support for both European integration and the Atlantic alliance. While the Dutch see the EU as an effective means of reining in nationalism, German and otherwise, they also know that the U.S. is ultimately the most reliable guarantor of their security. Reinforcing the Netherlands' Euroatlanticist orientation is its long and rich history of political, economic, and cultural links to nearby Britain. King William III of England (1650–1702) was a Dutchman, and Anglo-Dutch enterprises, of which Shell and Unilever are merely two of the best known, today account for many billions of dollars in annual business.

BRITISH ISLES

Great Britain and the Republic of Ireland

As the ancestral lands of tens of millions of American citizens, these island countries have a strong kinship with the U.S., with which they also share the bond of language. Ireland has an ambivalent relationship with its larger neighbor, to which it is in many senses closer than to continental Europe but with which it has yet to settle all the grievances accumulated during its centuries as a British colony. The two nations share a preference for free market economics but differ crucially in their basic foreign policy.

Economic Policy

Britain remains the most dynamic and successful of Europe's major economies, owing largely to the decision by Tony Blair's New Labour government, in power since 1997, to maintain the preceding Conservative governments' pro-business policies of privatization and deregulation. Blair has in recent years raised spending on public services, but the biggest burdens on British enterprise have been regulations mandated by Brussels. Britain's privatized pension system, in contrast to the publicly funded, pay-as-you-go systems that prevail on the continent, reduce the risk of future tax hikes.

Business finds an even more hospitable climate in Britain's smaller neighbor Ireland, where the top corporate tax rate is only 12.5 percent. Light regulation, with the notable exception of environmental protection, has been another major factor in the growth of the Irish economy, now 80 percent larger in real terms than a decade ago. Along with the advantage of an English-speaking workforce, these elements explain why Ireland receives more foreign investment per capita than any other EU nation and almost one-third of all U.S. investment in the EU. These are attractions that even Ireland's rigid national wage policy and high nonwage costs cannot outweigh.

Relations with the U.S.

Many volumes have been written about the "special relationship" between Britain and the United States. Britain was one of the founding members of NATO, and its traditional ambivalence toward European integration has stemmed in part from wariness of any commitments that might compete with the Atlantic alliance. America's foremost ally in the Second Gulf War and in the diplomatic confrontations that preceded it, Britain contributed the second-largest contingent of troops to the coalition in Iraq. Notwithstanding profound changes in both American and British societies since World War II, a common language, political culture, and economic philosophy all reinforce the special relationship today.

Ireland, which did not participate directly in World War II, is by tradition one of the EU's six neutral nations (along with Austria, Cyprus, Finland, Malta, and Sweden). Therefore it does not belong to NATO, yet it has considered participating in the formation of multinational EU "battle groups" for peacekeeping purposes. Its sympathies in international affairs are broadly pro-American, an inclination reinforced by the large and well-organized Irish-American community.

BULGARIA AND ROMANIA

These neighboring Balkan countries share a Black Sea coastline, a heritage of Ottoman rule well into the nineteenth century, and the experience of Communist dictatorship until 1989. Since the fall of Communism, they have both increasingly strengthened their ties to the West, joining the World Trade Organization and NATO among other groups. In 2005, the Commission approved the accession of both countries to the EU two years later, pending the implementation of reforms to fulfill the economic and political criteria for membership. At the same time, the Commission warned Romania in particular that its judicial system, local administration, and antitrust enforcement regime were not up to par and that the country must do more to combat corruption before it could join the club.

Economic Policy

Bulgaria has made great strides in privatizing state-owned assets and removing price controls, but its labor market remains strictly regulated. Corruption in Bulgaria's judiciary and other parts of the government constitute a serious drag on business. Romania's heavy regulatory regime is extremely opaque, with frequent unannounced changes and intricate red tape. Corruption in the Romanian judiciary and the bureaucracy is widespread, and a complicated tax regime and an unreliable legal system are among the significant unofficial barriers to foreign investment.

Relations with the U.S.

Since 1991, both countries have received hundreds of millions of dollars in development assistance from the U.S. under the Support for East European Democracies (SEED) Act. Romania was the first country to join NATO's "Partnership for Peace" defense cooperation framework, in 1994; and in 2004, both Romania and Bulgaria became full-fledged NATO members. Leaders of both countries signed the "Vilnius 10" letter in support of U.S. policy toward Iraq in 2003, and both nations have contributed troops to the U.S.-led coalition in Iraq.

CENTRAL EUROPE

Austria, Croatia, the Czech Republic, Hungary, Slovakia, Slovenia

These six countries, whose territories were once encompassed by the Austro-Hungarian empire which disappeared at the end of World War I, retain strong cultural ties with each other. They are also linked by "infrastructure, including railroads, roads and natural gas pipelines," and a common interest in defending the influence of smaller states in the EU.[1]

Austria seeks to act as the region's leader, a plausible role given its wealth and seniority in the EU, but this is likely to change. Even before the post-Communist states joined the EU, Austria had lowered its corporate tax rates to approach (though not to match) neighboring Slovakia's flat rate of 19 percent. As the post-Communist economies grow, we can expect that the whole region will experience increased pressure to liberalize.

The EU has officially recognized Croatia as a candidate for membership, though as of this writing no date for accession has been set, and negotiations have been seriously impeded by the government's failure to hand over General Ante Gotovina, suspected of war crimes against ethnic Serbs in the early 1990s.

Economic Policy

Austria's economy struggles not only with high taxes but with a slow and complex bureaucracy, elaborate regulations on environmental protection and retail sales, and an overburdened publicly funded pension system. The government reportedly discourages foreign investment in several industries, including transportation.

Croatia is still in a relatively early phase of liberalization, with high tariffs and nontariff barriers, substantial barriers to foreign investment, price controls on a wide range of products, and strict regulation of the labor market. One relative bright spot is pension reform; according to *The Economist*, Croatia has made more progress in this department than France or Germany.

Hungary was a regional pioneer in economic liberalization and the privatization of state-owned industry after the fall of Communism. But the government in Budapest has emulated the practice of several senior EU member states in retaining "golden shares" in privatized enterprises that it considers "strategic," to prevent their takeover by foreign investors. Progress has been slow in making Hungary's judiciary more efficient and eliminating corruption in the administrative bureaucracy.

Similar problems continue to plague the Czech Republic, whose economy is tangled in red tape, a problem aggravated by local variations in health and safety regulation and by the inadequate resources of the administrative bureaucracy. Czech President Vaclav Klaus is a firm economic liberal of the Thatcherite school (not to mention an outspoken Euroskeptic, whose lack of enthusiasm for the European constitution is shared by a significant portion of his countrymen), but recent governments have been unable to inspire the consensus to continue necessary structural reforms.

The Slovak Republic, the poorer half of the former Czechoslovakia, has been at the regional vanguard of liberalization since 1998, when a reformist government replaced the nationalists under Vladimir Meciar (who returned to office as the largely ceremonial head of state in 2004). Privatization and the removal of price controls have boosted foreign investment in many industries including banking. Slovakia's low taxes and low labor costs have helped make the country a regional center for automobile manufacturing, as major car makers from Western Europe and Asia have constructed plants there. The labor market is still far from liberalized, however. Inefficiency and corruption remain problems in both the judiciary and the bureaucracy.

Richest and most developed of the post-Communist countries, known as the "Switzerland of Eastern Europe" on account of its prosperity as well as its beautiful mountainous terrain, Slovenia has done the least to liberalize its economy. The government has resisted divesting itself of major holdings in several industries, including banking and insurance. Foreign investors still encounter significant legal and administrative barriers in broadcasting, transportation, and other industries. Foreign businesses can find it difficult to get permission to buy land. The labor markets remain rigidly regulated, courts and bureaucracy inefficient.

Relations with the U.S.

Austria committed itself to neutrality in the treaty that ended its occupation by the Soviet Union in 1955; and today it is one of six traditionally neutral countries in the EU (the others being Cyprus, Finland, Ireland, Malta, and Sweden). Therefore it does not belong to NATO but has agreed to contribute to the formation of multilateral EU "battle groups" for peacekeeping purposes.

Austria is actually the odd man out, rather than the regional leader, with respect to foreign policy. Hungary and the Czech Republic were, along with Poland, the first post-Communist countries to join NATO in 1999. Five years later, Slovakia and Slovenia also joined NATO. In early 2003, during the run-up to the Second Gulf War, leaders of all the region's countries except Austria signed public letters in support of U.S. policy toward Saddam Hussein. Later, the Czech Republic, Hungary, and Slovakia contributed troops to the coalition in Iraq. Croatia joined NATO's "Partnership for Peace" defense cooperation framework in 2001 and has been reorganizing its forces in accordance with NATO standards in the hope of joining in 2007.

EUROPEAN FREE TRADE ASSOCIATION (EFTA)

Iceland, Liechtenstein, Norway, Switzerland

EFTA was founded in 1960 to form a free trade area, as a looser alternative to the EU's predecessor organization, the European Economic Community. While Austria, Britain, Denmark, Finland, Ireland, and Sweden all eventually left EFTA for the EU, these four states have stayed put for diverse reasons.

Norway's abstention from the EU derives in part from a characteristically Scandinavian concern for national sovereignty (neighboring Sweden did not join the EU until 1995, and neither Sweden nor Denmark has adopted the common euro currency) but also from a desire to maintain control of its fish-rich coastal waters, which Norway would otherwise have to share with fisherman from all the EU member states.[2] Iceland, which has close economic and cultural ties to Norway, also seeks to protect its fishery resources.

Switzerland is a country generally wary of international entanglements and did not even join the United Nations until 2002 (though it has long hosted UN institutions on its soil). Many Swiss reject EU membership, with its common foreign and security policy and compulsory adoption of EU law, since that would mean the end of their traditions of neutrality in international disputes and of direct democracy by referendum. Yet in June 2005 Swiss voters opted to join the passport-free Schengen area, which includes thirteen EU countries, and to cooperate with the EU on asylum issues. Liechtenstein's close ties to Switzerland—the latter country handles almost all of the former's external relations—as well as a shared interest in preserving low taxes and strict banking secrecy laws, mean that it would probably follow Switzerland's lead with regard to EU membership.

All the EFTA members except Switzerland are members of the European Economic Area (EEA), which gives them access to the EU's single market in return for contributions to the EU's budget and adoption of all EU laws relating to the single market. Switzerland has preferred to negotiate a series of ad hoc agreements, giving it many of the same privileges without forcing it conform to all EU regulations on such matters as working hours or the 15-percent minimum rate of sales tax.

Economic Policy

Iceland, Liechtenstein, and Switzerland all rank in top category of "free" in the 2005 edition of the *Index of Economic Freedom*. Norway, by contrast, restricts foreign investment in many sectors, including financial services, mining, and media, and heavily regulates its pharmaceutical industry. Government expenditures consume more than a fifth of Norway's GDP, and more than a sixth of state revenues come from publicly owned property and businesses, including banks.

Relations with the U.S.

Norway is a NATO member whose ties to the U.S. are kept strong by a large and active Norwegian-American community. Since 1951, the U.S. has been responsible for the defense of Iceland, the only NATO member with no standing military of its own; and American forces man the NATO Naval Air Station at Keflavik, Iceland.

Despite its policy of neutrality, Switzerland joined NATO's "Partnership for Peace" defense cooperation framework in 1996. In the wake of 9/11, Switzerland declared al Qaeda illegal and has since frozen over $22 million in assets of persons and organizations linked to terrorism. Like Switzerland, Liechtenstein has in recent years increased efforts to prevent its banking system from being used for money laundering and other criminal purposes.

FRANCE AND GERMANY

Conflict between France and Germany devastated Europe twice in the first half of the twentieth century. After World War II, the so-called

"Franco-German axis," formalized in the 1963 Elysée treaty, served as the engine of European integration. Germany has long been willing to contribute its vast economic resources to the EU and to let France take the lead in European political affairs, in exchange for European acceptance of Germany's growing economic power.

In their opposition to the second Gulf War, the two nations presented a strikingly united face to the world. But many question whether the alliance of continental Europe's most powerful nations can survive the divergence of their economic and geopolitical orientations.

Economic Policy

France remains Europe's dirigiste economy par excellence, with a quarter of its workforce on the government payroll and state spending accounting for over half of GDP. A thirty-five-hour work week, imposed since 2000 on firms with more than nineteen employees, epitomizes France's regulatory mindset. In early 2005, yielding to pressure from business, the government finally allowed companies to opt out of the thirty-five-hour requirement with employee consent; but labor market rigidities remain a major factor in explaining the country's persistently high unemployment rates. The government monopolizes markets for electricity, natural gas, and rail transportation and holds "golden shares" in partially privatized enterprises, including Air France and France Telecom, to prevent their acquisition by foreign investors. Television and radio are required by law to broadcast specific amounts of French and European programming.

Germany's Social Democratic Chancellor Gerhard Schröder has had some success in liberalizing his country's labor market. In 2005, jobless benefits were restricted to increase incentives for the unemployed to seek work. Yet strict limits on firing continue to discourage employers from hiring. Nonwage labor costs amounting to a third of gross wages remain a severe drag on the economy. Many young Germans have told me of their desire to move to a freer environment such as the U.S. in order to fulfill their ambitions.

Other aspects of Germany's economy also call for liberalization. Publicly owned banks account for more than half of all savings deposits and more than a third of all loans. These regional and municipal government institutions are more interested in sustaining local enterprise than in making a profit. Putting so much of the nation's capital under such management inevitably produces market distortions.

Though both countries feature a high degree of government intervention in the economy, dirigisme is more firmly established in France, a nation whose political centralization stands in contrast to the regional distribution of powers under German federalism. An indication of Germany's greater potential for liberalization is that its Social Democratic chancellor has pushed more aggressively for pro-business reforms than France's center-right president has done.

Relations with the U.S.

France's ongoing effort to cast the EU as a counterweight to America, with France itself at the helm of the new superpower, has been a theme of this book. Before, during, and after the Second Gulf War, the Chirac government acted true to type, particularly in opposing U.S. positions at the UN and in NATO and in proposing an EU military headquarters separate from the NATO command structure.

The German government joined France in these moves, but within a year, Schröder was disavowing any Euro-Gaullist grand strategy. For Germany, alliance with the U.S. remains essential, not only as a means of reassuring its Central and Eastern European neighbors that it poses no threat but as protection for Germany itself against the future possibility of Russian aggression. In addition, Germany has no geopolitical superpower pretensions of the kind that still tempt France. Only the idea that an independent EU "pole" is necessary to restrain a bellicose U.S. could still tempt Germany to abandon its traditional Euroatlanticism.

GREECE AND CYPRUS

Colonists from Greece first settled on the island of Cyprus in the twelfth century B.C., and ever since the two countries have been intimately linked by trade, language, culture, and politics. Greece's centuries-old conflict with Turkey has naturally extended to Cyprus, which is only forty miles off the shores of Anatolia. In 1974 the island was divided between a Greek-speaking southern sector and a northern sector populated almost exclusively by ethnic Turks and occupied by Turkish army troops. The internationally recognized Republic of Cyprus, which controls the south, was admitted to the EU in 2004 without the northern sector (which Turkey alone recognizes as an independent state). As of this writing, attempts to negotiate a reunification of the island have still not succeeded.

Economic Policy

Although the Republic of Cyprus is closely allied with the government in Athens on many questions of foreign policy, above all with regard to Turkey, the two states have markedly different approaches to the economy.

The Greek government intervenes in the economy to a high degree even by European standards. Through state-owned businesses, it indirectly controls prices in a wide range of industries. State-owned banks account for about half of deposits and nearly half of loans. Investment by non-EU sources is discouraged in a number of industries, including mining, broadcasting, and transportation. The bureaucracy is highly inefficient, and the judiciary is largely under the control of the dominant political party. Regulations are complex and inconsistently applied and especially burdensome with regard to the labor market.

Cyprus, by contrast, offers an environment exceptionally favorable to business, with one of the lowest corporate tax rates in the EU and a government that encourages foreign investment in most industries. An entrepreneur can usually set up a business within a week, and a transparent bureaucracy facilitates regulatory compliance. Cyprus's judiciary is known for its independence from the government—a legacy, like its relatively liberal economic system, of eighty-two years as a British colony.

Relations with the U.S.

Greece has been a NATO member since 1952 and was a recipient of U.S. military aid until the early 1990s. American policy toward

Serbia, with which Greece shares the Orthodox religious tradition, was a source of tension in the 1990s; but the most serious potential difficulties in U.S.-Greek relations undoubtedly regard Turkey, a fellow NATO member and aspiring EU member state. Conflict between the two Mediterranean nations stems from the medieval rivalry of the Byzantine and Ottoman empires and today looms over the so-far intractable problem of a divided Cyprus.

British army bases occupy 3 percent of Cyprus, under the treaty that granted the nation its independence in 1960, making the island one of NATO's most important Mediterranean outposts. However, the Republic of Cyprus itself has a tradition of neutrality, and its first president, Archbishop Makarios III, was a leader of the "nonaligned" movement during the Cold War. Many Greek Cypriots resent America for its support of Turkey, and the Cypriot government has threatened to complicate Turkey's admission to the EU.

IBERIA

Spain and Portugal

Both countries joined the EU in the 1980s, shortly after emerging from decades under right-wing dictatorships. Both have strong Euroatlanticist leanings rooted in their histories as major colonial powers in the New World.

Economic Policy

Under the center-right premier José María Aznar, who governed from 1996 to 2004, Spain liberalized its markets in banking, energy, telecommunications, gas, and electricity and cut public spending as a percentage of GDP—measures that helped Spain post the fastest growth rate of the larger EU countries in the early part of the century. José Luis Zapatero, the Socialist who won the 2004 elections, has prudently left Aznar's economic reforms in place.

Unfortunately, the center-right did little to liberalize Spain's labor market, the most expensive in Europe as far as dismissal costs, with typical payments for a laid-off employee approaching twice his annual salary. Aznar's minimal cuts in personal and corporate taxes left Spain with rates above the EU average. Nor was the center-right averse to using its "golden shares" in privatized businesses to fend off foreign investment, such as a Dutch firm's attempted takeover of the former government phone monopoly in 2000. None of these are policies that the Socialists are apt to change. Spain's legal system remains glacially slow and its administrative bureaucracy is in many cases obstructionist.

Liberalization started later in Portugal than in Spain. In 2002, center-right Prime Minister José Manuel Barroso (President of the European Commission since 2004) oversaw a program of budget cuts and privatization which lowered the projected budget deficit by a third. More austerity measures followed the next year. However, the government still uses the state-owned Caixa Geral de Depósitos, Portugal's largest financial services firm, to fend off foreign takeovers of selected enterprises; and the law continues to limit non-EU ownership of airlines, television stations, and telecommunications firms. Inefficient courts, bureaucratic red tape, and rigid labor laws remain heavy burdens on Portuguese enterprise. When I visited in 2004, Finance Minister Manuela Ferreira Leite voiced her hope that the EU's cap on budget deficits (which France and Germany have flouted for several years in a row, but which smaller countries feel more pressure to respect) would allow the government to cut its bloated public payroll while letting Brussels take the blame.

Relations with the U.S.

Both Spain and Portugal were neutral in World War II. After the Allied victory, Generalísimo Francisco Franco's infamy from the bloody Spanish Civil War (1936–1939) and his obvious sympathy for Hitler left his regime a pariah. Spain did not join NATO until 1982, seven years after Franco's death. The dictatorship of António Salazar was considered mild enough that Portugal could join NATO as a founding member in 1949. Both countries hosted U.S. bases during the Cold War.

Spain's Premier Aznar led the "Group of Eight" European leaders who signed a public letter supporting U.S. Iraq policy early in 2003, and his country was one of the larger contributors of troops to the coalition forces. Then Aznar's successor Zapatero pulled Spanish troops out of Iraq within a month of taking office in 2004 and signaled that Spain's foreign policy would henceforth hew closer to the Franco-German line.

Whatever the policies of a particular government in Madrid, Spain is bound to remain fundamentally Euroatlanticist, for at least two historical reasons.

Like Britain, Spain has long had an ambivalent relationship with the rest of Europe. It is just as likely to identify with the Hispanic world in the Western Hemisphere, where Spanish corporations today have a growing economic presence and whence Spain draws a substantial number of low-wage immigrant workers. A small but influential group of opinion- and decision-makers in the mother country would like to see Spain reassume cultural leadership of the Spanish-speaking nations, including the growing Latino community in the United States.

The other reason for Spain's ambivalence toward Europe is its long-standing rivalry with neighboring France. Such a relationship might seem irrelevant in light of integration, but European nations have long memories and even more deeply rooted attitudes toward each other.

As for Portugal, its tradition of looking westward is even more pronounced than Spain's, in large part for the simple reason that it is an Atlantic country with no direct access to the Mediterranean. A long history of alliances and commercial relations with Britain have only reinforced this tendency. In 2003, then-Premier Barroso signed the pro-U.S. letter by the "Group of Eight" and hosted the historic summit of American, British, and Spanish leaders in the Azores on the eve of the Second Gulf War. Barroso's presidency of the European Commission thus augurs well for relations between the U.S. and the EU.

ITALY AND MALTA

Italy and Malta have economic and cultural ties that stretch back to ancient times, and these connections have been reaffirmed since Malta's independence from British colonial rule in 1964. Maltese is a Semitic language closely related to Arabic, yet it contains many elements of Sicilian dialect (as well as English). Italy and Malta both have strong economic and cultural ties to Libya, ties which they maintained even during the most aggressive phase of the Gadhafi dictatorship. As Malta's Foreign Minister John Dalli explained to me on my visit in 2004, the island nation sees itself as a potential bridge between Europe and the Muslim world.

Economic Policy

Despite some efforts at liberalization by the center-right government of Silvio Berlusconi, which took power in 2001, Italy's economy remains overregulated, especially with respect to the labor market. All but the smallest firms must effectively grant jobs for life, which naturally discourages hiring and thus reinforces structural unemployment. Italy's environmental laws, which reportedly number over 40,000, are inconsistently applied. Starting a business involves a daunting amount of red tape. The court system is notoriously inefficient, with the average time to final judgment on a civil suit nearly a decade. Government corruption is worse in Italy than in any other major industrialized country, and extortion by organized crime is common in the southern regions. The liabilities of Italy's state-funded pension system amount to 15 percent of the country's GDP, the highest proportion in the EU, while its fertility rate (and thus its future ratio of workers to retirees) is among the lowest.

Malta, on the other hand, has sound courts and a clear, efficient regulatory system. Establishing a business is a simple matter. The major obstacle to a free economy in Malta is the government's reluctance to privatize its holdings in several industries, including energy, where it maintains a virtual monopoly.

Relations with the U.S.

Since World War II, Italy has been an enthusiastic backer of European integration as well as a faithful ally of the U.S. Its Atlanticism is no doubt reinforced by the size of the Italian-American community, which has been estimated at 16 million U.S. citizens. Prime Minister

Berlusconi, who once quipped that he agreed with the American position on international issues "even before I know what it is," signed
the letter of the "Group of Eight" supporting U.S. Iraq policy in early
2003, and Italy was the third largest contributor of troops to the
coalition forces in Iraq. Italy's parliamentary opposition is less
ardently philo-American than Berlusconi, and a center-left government (which would probably be headed by former European
Commission President Romano Prodi) could weaken the country's
commitment to the Atlantic alliance.

Malta, a former British colony, has been officially nonaligned since
it left the British Commonwealth and became a republic in 1974. Its
strategic position and long history of close relations with nearby
Libya should prove valuable in the fight against Islamist terrorism.

POLAND

Poland, in my view, belongs in a category all by itself, because of its
links to so many different parts of the continent. If Europe is defined
to include Russia, then Poland lies smack in the center of the map.
(The geographic center of the present EU lies slightly west of the
Polish border, in eastern Germany.) Long the object and victim of
struggles between Russia and Germany, Poland knows keenly the
value of European peace. Its Slavic tongue links it to the East, its
Roman Catholic religion to the West. With a highly educated workforce and one of the EU's larger populations, Poland is bound to
become a major force in twenty-first-century Europe.

Economic Policy

Poland's "shock therapy" approach to liberalization in the early 1990s
was the first step in a steady process of reform that has made its economy one of the richest and freest among the post-Communist states.
The government still has a large presence in the banking and insurance sectors, but the biggest market-distorting influences are bureaucratic red tape, obscure regulations and tax laws, and, most seriously
of all, persistent corruption in the legal system.

Relations with the U.S.

Poland joined NATO in the first round of post-Communist enlargement in 1999. Four years later then–Prime Minister Leszek Miller signed the letter of the "Group of Eight" in support of U.S. Iraq policy, and Poland contributed the fourth-largest contingent of troops to the coalition forces in Iraq. Polish leaders have since voiced disappointment that their nation's businesses failed to receive favored treatment in the awarding of contracts for the rebuilding of Iraq, and that their citizens must still apply for visas in order to enter the U.S. Yet the nation's commitment to the Atlantic alliance remains basically strong. History has taught Poland to fear Russia and Germany, and to look beyond Europe for guarantees of its security.

SCANDINAVIA

Denmark, Finland, Sweden

The Scandinavian nations are among the best run and most successful in Europe and the world. With a long tradition of government benefits and social protections for their citizens, these countries have recently adopted economic reforms which they hope will make their expensive welfare states viable in the long run. Though not equally strong in their support for American policies, their democratic ideals and free trade principles make them natural partners for the U.S. on a wide range of international issues.

Economic Policy

Owing to the fame of Sweden's "cradle-to-grave" public services, Americans are apt to regard these countries as epitomes of the high-tax European welfare state. Many of us recall left-wing politicians and commentators in the 1960s and 1970s who held up Sweden as the model of a caring and generous society. We also remember news reports of prominent Swedes, such as the film director Ingmar Bergman, emigrating to avoid its exorbitant tax rates.

Today Scandinavian countries continue to provide their citizens with a wide range of publicly funded services, including medical care, education, and care for children and the elderly. Tax rates, while down from the confiscatory levels of a few decades back, are still among the highest anywhere. Yet the latest edition of the *Index of Economic Freedom* ranks the EU's three Scandinavian member states as among the world's freest economies. One, Denmark, rates an even higher ranking than the United States.

What explains this apparent contradiction? Although these countries are run by high-tax, big-spending regimes (with government expenditures ranging from half to nearly 60 percent of GDP, compared with 36 percent in the U.S.), other aspects of their economic landscape are highly conducive to business. Their judicial systems and civil services are paragons of efficiency, transparency, and honesty. Banking is wide open to foreign competition. Though regulation is generally heavier than in the U.S., especially with regard to environmental protection and the labor market, well-organized bureaucracies make compliance relatively easy. The legalities of setting up a business are simple, especially in Denmark and Sweden.

Scandinavian governments have started reforming some of the basic institutions of their welfare states. Sweden's top corporate tax rate is only 28 percent. Denmark has made its labor market far more flexible and recently started making a planned series of cuts in personal income tax. The general trend in the region is toward economic liberalization, making Scandinavia one part of the EU where it should get only easier and more profitable for Americans to do business.

Relations with the U.S.

Sweden and Finland are two of the EU's traditionally neutral nations. They are not members of NATO, but have chosen to contribute to the formation of multinational EU "battle groups" for peacekeeping purposes.

Denmark was a founding member of NATO in 1949. Its Prime Minister Anders Fogh Rasmussen signed the letter of the "Group of Eight" supporting U.S. Iraq policy in early 2003, and it has contributed troops to the coalition forces in Iraq.

TURKEY

Turkey has been an official candidate for EU membership since 1999, and in December 2004, the EU member states announced that accession negotiations would begin the following October. The negotiations are expected to last at least a decade and are highly controversial within the EU itself (see chapter 5). When I visited Turkey in late 2004, the political, intellectual, and business leaders I met spoke passionately of their desire to establish their country's European credentials by qualifying for membership in the EU. At the same time, many thought that the political and economic reforms demanded by Brussels would be their own reward and that in the end, Turkey might be better off remaining an EU affiliate instead of a full-fledged member, enjoying access to the single market, yet retaining the freedom to act as an economic and geopolitical bridge between East and West.

Economic Policy

Turkey has been lowering its tariffs on foreign goods but protects many domestic industries with quotas and outright prohibitions on imports. The law restricts foreign investment in several industries including broadcast media, aviation, and telecommunications. Red tape, capricious bureaucrats, and low-level corruption are significant drags on economic activity. The government dominates the banking industry and controls the prices of pharmaceuticals and many crops. The *Index of Economic Freedom* rates the Turkish economy as "mostly unfree."

Relations with the U.S.

Turkey has been a NATO member since 1952, and according to the U.S. State Department, "serves as [NATO's] vital eastern anchor," since it controls the straits between the Black Sea and the Mediterranean and shares a border with Syria, Iraq, and Iran. Ankara's refusal in 2003 to let American troops cross its territory into Iraq was a significant strain on relations, yet Turkey remains a key ally. The U.S. has long supported Turkish membership in the EU, a position which has more than once provoked irritation in European leaders. When President George W. Bush expressed this view in 2004, French President Jacques Chirac retorted that "it was a bit as if I were to tell Americans how they should handle their relationship with Mexico."

Notes

1. "EU: A New Voting Bloc," Strategic Forecasting, LLC, http://www .stratfor.com, June 28, 2004.
2. "The Norwegian Option," *The Economist*, October 7, 2004.

Acknowledgments

IN PREPARING this book, I benefited from the observations of many officials and former officials of the European institutions, including the former commissioners Frits Bolkestein, Viscount Etienne Davignon, Lord Kinnock (Neil Kinnock), Erkki Liikanen, Lord Patten of Barnes (Chris Patten), and António Vitorino. Pat Cox, former president of the European Parliament, and two members of Parliament, Hans-Gert Poettering and James Elles, provided insight into that increasingly important legislative body. My fellow ambassadors Thom de Bruijn and Umberto Vattani shared their crucial perspectives as permanent representatives of EU member states in Brussels.

No less valuable were comments from outside experts on the EU institutions: Susan Danger, William Drozdiak, Ambassador Jeremy Kinsman, Maria Laptev, Ambassador Richard Morningstar, Professor Robert A. Mundell, Martin Porter, Jürgen Strube, and Maja Wessels.

The experts on the staff of the U.S. Mission to the European Union were of invaluable help with this project, as they were with my day job in Brussels. James J. Foster, deputy chief of mission for most of my tenure; his successor P. Michael McKinley; and John Sammis, minister-counselor for economic affairs, all kindly read the manuscript in draft form and much improved it with their suggestions. Rick Holtzapple, Todd Huizinga, Jonathan Kessler, Pat Lerner, Lee Litzenberger, Harry O'Hara, Van Reidhead, Mark Richard,

Michael C. Ryan, Kyle Scott, Frederick Wilson, and Christopher S. Wilson were all willing and able to discuss their areas of specialization in terms accessible to the intelligent lay reader. Their knowledge enriches this book, while any errors are the responsibility of my coauthor and myself.

Here is also a good place to thank my chiefs of staff, Megan Marshall and Margaret C. Dickerson; my executive assistant Judith S. Moore; and Sarah L. Groen, of the embassy's Office of Political Affairs, for their excellent and tireless service.

Thanks to Csaba T. Chikes for his suggestions on further reading and to Muriel Van Averbeke for facilitating my coauthor's visit to the European Parliament.

Friends who helped make this book possible include Ambassador George L. Argyros, Keiko Foster, and Michael Gonzalez.

I would like to thank my literary agents Greg Dinkin and Frank R. Scatoni, my attorney Jacqueline Davies, and my editor Christopher A. Anzalone for all their fine and patient work.

My coauthor Frank Rocca thanks James Graff, Charles Hill, Jeff Israely, and Barry Lynham for their help in understanding Europe and transatlantic relations; Greg Dinkin and Frank Scatoni for selling the book with flair; Chris Anzalone and Lynn Weber for editing it while fielding countless changes; Mike Gonzalez for bringing author and coauthor together and for his suggestions on research; Mike Vaccaro for bringing authors and agents together; and Simon Frankel for his legal counsel. Frank would like to express his gratitude to Joaquín González-Alemán, John Lilly, and Vanessa Lilly for their *disponibilità*; to Justin Stares, Rob Stone, and Web Stone for guidance at various critical points in the project; to Wlady Pleszczynski for his constant moral and intellectual support; and to his family, particularly to his brother Lawrence Rocca and his wife Vitamaria Bosco for their help and encouragement from start to finish.

Finally, I would like to thank my own family, especially my wife Marna, for her careful reading of the manuscript and her assistance in countless other ways. Our three children, their spouses, and our four grandchildren provided long-distance inspiration from California for this effort to help bridge the gap between Europe and America.

Index

About the Authors

ROCKWELL A. SCHNABEL was the United States ambassador to the European Union from 2001 to 2005; ambassador to Finland under President Ronald Reagan; and deputy secretary of commerce under President George H. W. Bush. A longtime businessman, he is chairman and cofounder of Trident Capital, a venture capital firm, and was president of the brokerage firm Bateman Eichler Hill Richards (now Wachovia Bank). Ambassador Schnabel was born in the Netherlands, where he attended Trinity College. He lives in Los Angeles.

(All of his proceeds from this book will go to endow the Rockwell Anthony Schnabel Award for Advancing U.S.-EU Relations, which recognizes outstanding efforts in advancing U.S. policy objectives through cooperation with the EU.)

FRANCIS X. ROCCA is an American journalist based in Rome. He has written about European business, politics, and culture for the *Wall Street Journal*, *Time*, *The Spectator* (London), *Forbes*, the *Chronicle of Higher Education*, the *Atlantic Monthly*, and the *American Spectator*, among other publications. A former Fulbright fellow in Spain, he is a graduate of Gonzaga College High School, Harvard College (A.B.), St. John's College, Annapolis (M.A.), and Yale University (Ph.D.).